Pigeon Prayers

And

Praises

A Collection of Christian Poetry

By

Mary Ahlstrom Palmquist

Scriptures marked NIV are taken from the NEW INTERNATIONAL VERSION (NIV): Scripture taken from THE HOLY BIBLE, NEW INTERNATIONAL VERSION ®. Copyright© 1973, 1978, 1984, 2011 by Biblica, Inc.™. Used by permission of Zondervan

Copyright © 2019 Mary Palmquist

All rights reserved. No part of this publication may be reproduced, stored in a retrieval system, or transmitted in any form or by any means, electronic, mechanical, photocopying, recording, or otherwise, without the prior written permission of the publisher.

ISBN: 978-1-60383-584-8
Published by:
Holy Fire Publishing
www.HolyFirePublishing.com

Cover Design: Jay Cookingham

Printed in the United States of America, The United Kingdom and Australia

PREFACE

There are many types of pigeons. In Bible times, still under the old covenant, they were used as sacrifices. Today many domesticated pigeons are trained to carry messages much like Jesus' disciples and the Apostle Paul and his partners. Homing pigeons always return home to their master or trainer. Likewise, Christians look forward to going home to the mansions prepared for them in heaven (John 14:2). A study in Current Biology 2017 reports that pigeons can find their way home from 1300 miles away. Somehow they understand the concept of both time and space. Their navigational skills made pigeons great long-distant messengers during World Wars I and II, they saved thousands of human lives. 200,000 pigeons were at the disposal of the American military.

God is in the business of saving lives and we are his messenger pigeons. In an article in Star Tribune, Jim Williams writes, "I love the way flocks of pigeons fly. They swoop and glide, pump up speed, then float. They circle, they soar. Pigeons display the pure joy of flying. They fly like they're having fun. God meant for Christians to have the same flying experiences." Jesus said, "I have come that they might have life, and have it abundantly." John 10:10b RSV

Homing pigeons and Messenger Pigeons are obedient. They have been trained to be obedient. Christians are in obedience training all their lives, and often don't learn nearly as quickly as pigeons. "And this is love, that we walk (or fly) in obedience to God's commands." I John 6a NIV (Paraphrase mine)

DEDICATION

This book is dedicated to my brother, Charlie Ahlstrom, who has raised and trained pigeons since he was a teenager. He and our other brothers acquired pigeons mostly under bridges, and occasionally in church belfries. Pigeons go to church too! I hope he enjoys my version of praying and praising pigeons!

ACKNOWLEDGMENTS

Thank you to the following friends, who eagerly proofread, encouraged, and who also advised me on the selection of poetry for this book: Jynane Staley, Nicole Dewes, Emily Dewes, and Dorrie Johnson. I love you all! I also want to give a big thank-you to my Bible study groups who are always overflowing with wisdom, solid inspiration, and sincere encouragement. They are the salt of the earth! Additionally, I owe a debt of gratitude to all the Christian pastors, leaders, mentors, writers and colleagues who have ministered to me through the years. Special thanks to Winnie Kunz who led me into a personal relationship with Jesus Christ. Bless them all; they put up with all my questions and outspoken opinions.

My purpose in publishing this book of poetry is to honor and glorify God, who is my sole inspiration for writing. I have been writing poetry since I was 12. And now, at the advanced age of 82, I am experiencing a dream come true. Thank you God!

"Who knows better than he how to guide our mind and pen for His design?"

-John Bunyan

TABLE OF CONTENTS

Preface	i
Dedication	ii
Acknowledgements	iii
Trumpeter Pigeons (Praying Pigeons)	16
Persevere	17
Plastic Faith?	18
A Fool for Christ	19
Questions	20
humble priest	21
Master of the Harvest	24
Broken Pottery	26
Mystery	27
Scrub the Smudge	28
Loose and Bind; In Bethlehem	29
Breathe on me Breath of God	30
Vessel of Blessing	31
Make My Light Shine	32
Be My Strength	33
From His Perspective	34
Keep it Burning!	35
How Did I Live My Life Today?	36
Grow Me, Lord!	37
Mysteries	38
Lord, Be There	39
Adrift	40
Make Me a Light	42
Wideness in Your Mercy	43

Life is a Prayer	44
Why, Lord ?	45
Tender My Heart	46
Pound Him with Your Spirit	47
Holy Words	48
Lord, Release Me	49
Purify	50
Whisper Your Words	51
Hot or Cold	52
Puzzled Pieces Prayer	53
Splinters of Deceit	54
Appointing My Days	55
Treasures	56
Praising Pigeons	57
Upon my Altar of Praise	58
April Dawn	59
Morning Prayer	60
Suffering into Praise	61
Oh, My Jesus, I Love You	62
I Found My Joy in Jesus	63
Showers of Blessings	64
His Rain	65
I Am the One	66
Holy Be His Name	67
A Crown in Heaven	68
Shout Hallelujah!	69
Rejoice in the Lord	70
The Dance	71
Fantail Pigeons	72

Ella	73
Emma	74
Living Waters	75
Rainbow Grace	76
Son, Are You Ready to Fly?	77
Galaxy of Grace	78
A Bible of My Own	79
Jody	80
Everlasting	82
Signature of Heaven	83
Music of Heaven	84
Let the Children Come	85
The Pharisee and the Publican	86
Inheritance from God	87
Abba, Father, God!	89
Mighty Magnet	90
Lily Pads on Loon Lake	91
Assembly of Driftwood	92
Kathleen at 99	94
Grace	95
Stranger-Friend	96
The Christening	97
This I Know	98
Vanity	99
Pulpit Pigeons	**100**
Can't Take it with You	101
Set Your Hand to the Plow	102
Covenant God	103
Faithful in Small Things	104

Joy Comes in the Morning	105
Come!	106
He Knew	108
Whoever Has Ears, Listen!	109
All is Well	110
Jubilee!	111
I Was the Woman	113
Jesus Explosion	115
Ever-Green	116
I Don't Know Your Mary	117
Awesome Reach	119
Child of Mine	120
Is Anything Too Hard for God?	121
Bethlehem of Judah	122
Trust and Obey	123
Whispering Thoughts	124
Mary's Child	125
Come Walk with Me	126
Remedy for Sin	127
Sooooo Big!	128
Sweet Peace	129
Resting in Jehovah	130
Wandering	131
Peace Beyond Understanding	132
Our God is Not a Wasteful God	133
Fear Not Little Flock	134
The Log	135
Are You Walking with Jesus?	137
Damascene Pigeons (New Beginnings)	138

New Beginning	139
Pruning	140
Occupation	141
The Second Mile	144
The Master Mender	146
From Glory unto Glory	148
He Leadeth Me	150
Higher Math	152
The House of the Lord	153
I Am the One	154
Holy of Holies	155
God is Living	156
Hungry Pigeons (and thirsty, too!)	**157**
Fishing with Jesus	158
Very Pregnant	159
A Glutton for Living Water	160
Needy	161
New Year	162
You Speak to Me in Poetry	163
Questions	164
Thy Word	165
The Wine of Your Word	166
More of Jesus	167
Living Words	168
My Joy is Leaking, Lord	169
Tree of Life	170
The Hem of His Garment	171
I Want to See Your Face	172
Emmaus Road	173

Leavened Bread	174
Rock Pigeons	175
He is My Rock	176
Solid Foundation	177
Give Us Grace to Stand	178
Josephine	179
Rock of Salvation	181
Helmet Pigeons	182
A Christian with a Mission	183
Forward into Battle	184
Hope `a la King	185
The Battle is the Lord's	186
The Armor of God	187
A Shell-tered Life	188
Save Us from this Hour	189
A Just Survivor	190
Battle of the Mind	191
Archangel Pigeons	192
Christmas Blessings	193
Overanxious	194
Cowboy Boots in Heaven	195
In Your Will?	196
First and Foremost	197
Instant Gratification	198
Doing the Polka in Heaven	199
King Pigeons	200
Transcending Sound	201
You are My Everything	202
The Great I Am	203

Gathering Time	204
stillborn syllables	205
Death	206
Running Free	207
Dustin	208
Molly	209
Dustin and Molly	210
Brooding Silence	211
Sanctuary	212
Dark Winter	213
Sharing Seeds	214
Loaves and Fishes	215
Sprinkle Me Softly	216
I Walked With Death Today	217
Slow Journey	218
Pouter Pigeons	**219**
Pouter Pigeons	220
When Did You Make Them That Way?	221
No Room	222
Crossed Emotions	223
Consider the Pussy Willow	225
Pride	226
Homing Pigeons (Homing, Racing, & Messenger)	**228**
Ordinary People	229
Motherhood	230
The Postman Cometh	231
One Guest Room	232
My Strength	233
Fruit Patches	234

Lost	235
Without Restraint	237
The Wind Blows Where It Will	238
Dearest Babe of Bethlehem	239
Nine-Eleven	240
Coming Home	241
Footprints	243

People Pigeons

Pigeon families differ
greatly from each other,
come in different sizes,
and many different colors.

Plump or slender they can be,
fancy, vibrant, plain.
They may not respond to you,
when called their species name.

Nesting habits, not the same,
don't always flock together.
Some will shiver in the rain;
others brave the weather.

Some are dirty; some quite clean,
they function differently.
Some are trained with special skills
while others – no degree!

One thing they have in common;
this I can't deny.
God gave each a pair of wings
and taught them how to fly!

"But those who hope in the Lord will renew their strength. They will soar on wings like eagles; they will run and not grow weary, they will walk and not faint."
Isaiah 40:31 NIV

Trumpeter Pigeons (Praying Pigeons)

Trumpeters are show birds, not raised for flight. These birds were named for their peculiar call, which is louder than that of other pigeons. It is a continuous rising and falling, almost drum-like sound. Another major characteristic of the breed are its boots. A Trumpeter's foot and hock feathers can reach up to 8 or 10 inches. This does not make for a very aerodynamic bird. When I got Ptarmigan, it was several months before he developed the wing strength to fly to the top of the barn with the other pigeons – and if there was any wind, he was in real trouble. He learned to walk on windy days! **Used by permission of Barry Koffler. Feathersite.com**

The Bible tells us to "pray without ceasing." We are much like the Trumpeters in this respect. We can pray about anything and everything with soft or loud voices, tears or laughter, and God will hear and answer our prayers. We can whisper or shout our prayers; sometimes God will shout out his answer. Other times we might barely hear him. In order to readily hear God's voice, we must develop the art of listening. We are grounded by gravity, and the Trumpeters are grounded by their long feathered boots, but our prayers will fly! James, the brother of Jesus, reminds us that "the prayer of a righteous person is powerful and effective." James 5:16 NIV Join the circle of Trumpeters!

Persevere

"I will strike the shepherd
And the sheep will scatter." *

When I needed comfort,
You chose to run, not gather.
I was the shepherd of your flock;
You always knew my voice.
When I called, you followed.
It was a covenant of choice.

I gladly gave you comfort,
Provided you with rest.
You took my yoke upon you;
I was pleased to do the rest.
I gathered you, my little chicks
And sheltered you from harm.
I kept you safe within the boat;
I spoke to wind and storm.

I taught you all that I received
From my Father-God.
I gave you power to heal the sick,
I gave my staff and rod.
Bumps and jolts along the road
Soon caused you all to fear.
You fled my side; you wandered off;
You chose not to appear.

I hung alone; I died alone;
None of you came near.
You denied the crucified;
You could not persevere

*Hebrews 14:27b, Zechariah 13

"You need to persevere so that when you have done the will of God, you will receive what he promised...my righteous one will live by faith, and I take no pleasure in the one who shrinks back." Hebrews 10:36,38a NIV

Plastic Faith?

Are you walking on the water
With arms outstretched to me,
While deepening darkness lingers,
And your shadow I can't see?

Am I clinging to my little boat,
Afraid to take a risk?
Do I have a plastic faith,
Just like a floppy disc?

Do I waiver, Lord, in courage;
Safe in the boat of self?
Am I failing to explore
Your precious water wealth?

Then call me from this coward boat;
To feel the water swell.
Keep in mind, my precious Lord,
That I don't hear so well.

"They mounted up to the heavens and went down to the depths; in their peril their courage melted away. They reeled and staggered like drunkards; they were at their wits' end. Then they cried out to the Lord in their trouble, and he brought them out of their distress. He stilled the storm to a whisper; the waves of the sea were hushed, and he guided them to their haven. Psalms 107:26-30 NIV

A Fool for Christ

Can I be a fool for Christ,
store my treasures up in heaven?
Can I forgive not seven times,
but foolishly, seventy times seven?

Can I truly love my enemies,
forgive all those who hate me?
Pray for those who persecute,
who torment and berate me?

Can I turn the other cheek
when insults mock my faith?
Can I lose my life for him
And keep my pathways straight?

I WILL be a fool for Christ;
I'll dance before his throne!
I WILL be a fool for Christ
And call his Kingdom Home.

"But God chose the foolish things of the world to shame the wise; God chose the weak things of the world to shame the strong. He chose the lowly things of this world and the despised things—and the things that are not—to nullify the things that are."
1 Corinthians 27-28 NIV

Questions

Lord, you know I'm full of questions
about your holy Word.
The world is full of answers,
that do not go unheard.

Answers parade before me,
all having bits of truth.
Still seeking more, I agonize;
it's like an aching tooth!

You can ease that aching tooth;
the process is most frugal.
Child of questioning agony,
have you not heard of Google?

"Be patient toward all that is unresolved in your heart. Try to love the questions themselves. Do not now seek the answers, which cannot be given because you would not be able to live them. And the point is to live everything. Live the questions now. Perhaps you will then gradually, without noticing it, live along some distant day into the answers."--Rainer Maria Rilke

"Blessed are those who find wisdom, those who gain understanding, for she is more profitable than silver and yields better returns than gold." Proverbs 3:13-14 NIV

humble priest

I'm listening for your voice today;
take my hand and lead the way.
Don't let me miss a single word;
I want to hear you speak, oh Lord.

Lest I should walk in my own will;
instruct me. Lord, I will be still.
In thankfulness I offer praise;
my heart and hands, in love, I raise.

Then may your voice be loud and clear;
render peace and calm my fear.
Again, I promise to be still;
just let me know and do your will.

I'm listening Lord, what did you say?
Oh, yes, I'll serve the Lord today.
What's that, dear Lord, I didn't hear;
please speak again, I'm standing near.

You say that you've anointed me
A humble priest, how can that be?
Oh, precious Lord, you must explain;
I thought a priest must be a man.

Oh, yes, I do; I love you, Lord,
and how I love your holy Word!
You say I must to others show
the love and joy and peace I know,

and the source from which it came,
bringing glory to your name?
Thank you, Lord, for now I know;
I will that love to others show.

To you, oh Lord, I do belong.
When I am weak, then am I strong.
In your kingdom, though I'm least,
Yes, I will be your humble priest.

"As you come to him, the living stone – rejected by humans but chosen by God and precious to him – you, also, like living stones, are being built into a spiritual house to be a holy priesthood, offering spiritual sacrifices acceptable to God through Jesus Christ. For in the Scripture it says: See, I lay my stone in Zion, a chosen and precious cornerstone, and the one who trusts in him will never be put to shame."
1 Peter 2:4-6 NIV

Man of Sorrows

Man of sorrows, bruised and bloody,
comfort all who suffer loss.
Help them leave their wounded spirits
safe, secure beneath your cross.

Raise them up from burning ashes;
turn their hearts toward words of grace.
Man of sorrows, bruised and bloody,
renew their faith on wings of peace.

Friend of Sinners, take their burdens;
fling them far beyond the seas.
Swallow up their guilt and sorrow;
replace with joy and praise to thee.

Lifter-up of hands toward heaven,
receive our prayer and praise on high.
Comfort, comfort we your people;
bring your holy kingdom nigh.

"But he was wounded for our transgressions, He was bruised for our iniquities; upon him was the chastisement that made us whole; and with his stripes we are healed." Isaiah 53:5 RSV

"'Comfort, comfort now my people; tell of peace,' so says our God. 'Comfort those who sit in darkness, mourning under sorrow's load.'"

Hymn: "Comfort, Comfort Now My People" Text: Johann Olearius, Tune: Trente quatre de David

Master of the Harvest

Dear Master of the harvest,
teach me to sow your wheat,
that I may reap a bounty
as I sow the golden seed.

I'm an inexperienced farmer, Lord,
yet zealous to succeed.
So walk me through the process,
and help me sow the wheat.

"Don't let the seed fall on the path
that many walk upon,
for surely birds will snatch it up,
or man will trample on.

You see those rocks beyond us there?
Do not be deceived.
Though seed may sprout, it cannot live –
No moisture to believe.

And never sow among the thorns.
Their prickly, stickly stems
will suffocate the struggling seed
and choke the life within.

But HERE, beloved, is the place;
in good soil, let it fall.
Faith will increase in open hearts,
Who hear the harvest call."

"Some people are like seed sown along the path, where the word is sown. As soon as they hear it, Satan comes and takes away the Word that was sown in them. Others, like seed sown on rocky places, hear the word and at once receive it with joy. But since they have no root, they last only a short time. When trouble or persecution comes because of the Word, they quickly fall away. Still others, like seeds sown among the thorns, hear the word, but the worries of this life, the deceit-fullness of wealth and the

desire and the desire for other things come in and choke the word, making it unfruitful. Others, like seed sown on good soil, hear the word, accept it, and produce a crop....some thirty, some sixty, and some a hundred times what was sown."
Luke 8:5-15 Mark 4:15-20 NIV

Broken Pottery

I was like broken pottery,
But you put me together again,
Blowing away my crippling pain
With the winds of righteousness.
Thank you almighty God!

I have waited on you, Lord,
Not always patiently,
But nevertheless,
You have made me to soar like the eagle.
Bringing me to new heights
And new flight patterns.
Praise you, almighty God!

You have ended my misery
And restored my soul
With healing in my wings.
Thank you almighty God!
I rest now in your everlasting love and favor!

"Praise the Lord, oh my soul, and forget not all his benefits—who forgives all your sins and heals all your diseases, who redeems your life from the pit and crowns you with love and compassion, who satisfies your desires with good things so that your youth is renewed like the eagle's. Psalms 103:1-5 NIV

Mystery

Oh God of the universe you are a mystery,
One I will never unravel, but long with all my heart to do so.
You give me exceeding great joy one day;
excessive pain, the next.

You say "Ask and you will receive."
I ask, and ask, and ask,
But sometimes the answers seem
trapped between heaven and earth.

You say, "Knock, and the door shall be opened."
Sometimes all doors are closed to me.

You say, "Seek and you shall find."
Sometimes you seem to hide yourself incredibly well;
You tell me whatever I ask will be done by my Father in Heaven;
I often grow anxious and weary trying to understand
Just what your answer is.

Your thoughts are not my thoughts;
Nor your ways mine, it is true.
They are fathoms higher and magnitudes mightier.

Father, I have accepted this in my questioning heart,
Knowing you are with me in every mystery
And will not fail me ever.
I don't need to unravel mysteries;
For I know you are in control.

I need to seek your face!
You will do the rest.

"...you will find him if you seek him with all your heart and all your soul..."
Deuteronomy 4:29b NIV

Scrub the Smudge

Who may ascend the mountain of God?
Who may stand in His holy place?
Do I have clean hands and a pure heart?
What does it take to see your face?

I was made in your image, I know.
Do I always reflect your light?
Do I demonstrate love wherever I go?
Have I smudges suppressing your sight?

Little white lies are not really small
Nor can I say they are white.
Coming straight from Adam's grave fall.
They are black with sin in his sight.

Judging others, a smudge on my heart,
That needs to be scrubbed and removed.
Shine in the corners and dig out the dirt
Of pride that hides in the grooves.

Scrub the smudges from me, oh Lord;
And if the smudges don't budge,
Stir your Spirit in me; sound the harpsichord;
I may need just one more nudge.

"Who may ascend the mountain of the Lord? Who may stand in his holy place? The one who has clean hands and a pure heart, who does not trust in an idol or swear by a false God. Such is the generation of those who seek him, who seek your face, God of Jacob." Psalm 24:3-4, 6 NIV

Loose and Bind In Bethlehem

Loose the joints and muscles, Lord, that bind;
Penetrate the pains of humankind.
Chase away the sorrow in this season;
Let there be no suffering without reason.
Loose the evil hatred and the lies;
Stamp out all the vengeance that defies.
Open wide the doors of doubtful hearts;
Show them where a grateful spirit starts.

Bind the joy of heaven everywhere;
Bind the hearts in worship and in prayer.
Let them know that Jesus came to save;
Tell them that the Babe has come to stay.
Let them see the star of Bethlehem;
Bind them to the carols and the hymns.
Bind them to the Christ child with a sigh.
Bind them to the manger, there to lie.

"Whatever you bind on earth will be bound in heaven, and whatever you loose on earth will be loosed in heaven." Matthew 16:19b NIV

Breathe on me Breath of God

Breathe on me breath of God,
gentleness and love,
each wisp of air for me to share
your mercies from above.

Breathe on me breath of God,
ancient wisdom true,
that I might speak, and not be meek,
on golden tongues for you.

Breathe on me breath of God,
spew out justice rare,
that I may fight to shine your light,
and strive for what is fair.

Breathe on me breath of God;
warm me with your glory.
Wake up my faith, increase my pace,
and please God, would you hurry?

"and with that he breathed on them and said, 'Receive the Holy Spirit.'" John 20:22 NIV

"…so that you may live a life worthy of the Lord and please him in every way…being strengthened with all power according to his glorious might so that you may have great endurance and patience…" Colossians 1:10a, 11 NIV

Vessel of Blessing

I am your vessel Lord,
designed for your glory.
Fill me to overflowing
with wisdom and knowledge.

Rain down upon me the mysteries of heaven.
Dip me deep in the rivers of mercy and love,
streams of righteousness,
cleansing waters of forgiveness.

Widen the walls of my vessel;
stretch the dimensions of faith.
Shower me with surprise,
flood me with peace in your presence;

Make the waters to rise
and overflow boundaries
that I might bless others
as you have blessed me.

"But we have this treasure in earthen vessels to show that the transcendent power belongs to God and not to us." 2 Corinthians 4:7 RSV

"Yet, O Lord, thou art our Father; we are the clay and thou art our potter; we are all the work of thy hand." Isaiah 64:8 RSV

Make My Light Shine

Oh God, make my little light shine,
a steady reflection of your love divine.
Shine like the brilliance of stars in the heaven,
like bright polished gems to the universe given.

Shine in the darkness of evil decay;
light up the pathways of truth and the way.
Shine with the radiance of love in your name;
shine with forgiveness, alleviate pain.

Oh God, make my little light shine,
in splendor before and behind.
Lighten up lives with words that adorn;
share my experience of new life reborn.

Shine in the corners of fear and defeat;
light from your source will never deplete.
Sing IN my joy; Shout OUT the dark;
Ring in your glory, let shadows depart.

Oh God, let my little light shine,
an accented statement, a heavenly sign.
I could go on foot, but light travels faster.
May your glorious light be my only true Master.

"The sun will no longer be your light by day, nor will the brightness of the moon shine on you, for the Lord will be your everlasting light, and your God will be your glory." Isaiah 60:19 NIV

Be My Strength

Don't only GIVE me strength, Lord,
But, BE the strength in me!
Break me of excuses,
 empty strength decrees.

Strength to lead your people
 from slavery into free;
I want the strength of Moses,
 with a heart for only thee.

Strength to topple Jerichos,
 walls to tumble down.
Strength to slay my giants;
 knock them to the ground.

Strength like Daniel praying
 while in the lion's den.
You were his saving strength;
You were his loud "amen."

Use the weakness of my flesh
 to glorify your name.
When I am weak, I will be strong;
Your living Word I claim.

"But he (Christ) said to me, 'My grace is sufficient for you, for my power is made perfect in weakness.' Therefore I will boast all the more gladly about my weaknesses, so that Christ's power may rest on me. That is why, for Christ's sake, I delight in weaknesses, in insults, in hardships, in persecutions, in difficulties. For when I am weak, then am I strong." 2 Corinthians 12:9-10 NIV

From His Perspective

Lift me high above the world;
let me see from your perspective,
breaking hearts and untold sorrow,
those who cannot face tomorrow.

Suffering souls who need your comfort,
lift me high so I can see
hopeless hearts that need compassion,
craving love that's everlasting.

Lift me high above the world,
show me how to be effective;
where to spread your holy Word,
seeking those who've never heard.

Hungry hearts that need salvation,
llft me high so I can see
thirsty lips for living water;
send me to your sons and daughters.

Lifted high above the world,
now I can see from your perspective,
all the needs beneath me swirl;
now put me back into the world.

"I pray that the eyes of your heart may be enlightened in order that you may know the hope to which he has called you, the riches of his glorious inheritance in his holy people, and his incomparably great power for us who believe. That power is the same as raised Jesus Christ from the dead and seated him at his right hand in the heavenly realms." Ephesians 1:18-20 NIV

Keep it Burning!

Put more oil in my lamp,
keep it burning,
burning, burning.
Put more oil in my lamp, I pray.

I need more energy,
more saving power from thee;
light my lamp,
oh, my Lord,
keep it burning.

Heavy are my arms, Lord;
leaden are my feet.
I find myself surrendering to defeat.
My oil is leaking fast; I know it will not last.
Light my little lamp, Lord, keep it burning.

Burning fire inside
to lift me and to guide,
pour the oil of gladness into me;
Light my path so I can see.
Keep it burning, Lord God, keep it burning.

I want to be prepared
for warfare everywhere;
do not let my weakness hinder me.
Raise me up, light my lamp;
keep it burning!

"You, Lord, keep my lamp burning; my God turns my darkness into light. With your help I can advance against a troop; with my God I can scale a wall." Psalms 18:27-28 NIV

"Be dressed and ready for service and keep your lamps burning for service." Luke 12:35 NIV

How Did I Live My Life Today?

How did I live my life today?
Did I trust? Did I obey?
Did I open up your Word?
Did I seek to serve You, Lord?

Did I turn to you in prayer?
Did I listen? Ears aware?
Did I seek the things above?
Did I accept and share your love?

Did I praise and worship you?
Did I consider what you'd do?
Did I choose the better part?
Or did I sorely miss the mark?

"…but seek first his kingdom and his righteousness…" Matthew 6:33b NIV

Grow Me, Lord !

Grow me in surrender, Lord,
To you, almighty King.
Grow me swift in patience
And waiting on your wing.

Grow me wide in wisdom, Lord,
Of your mysterious Word.
Grow me deep in faithfulness;
All my distractions curb.

Grow the fruit of gratitude;
Sink the roots of faith.
Fertilize obedience;
Water it with grace.

Grow me gentle, grow me strong;
Expand your love in me.
Grow me humble, shrink my pride
That I more clearly see.

Plant your truth; make it grow
High and green and ripe.
Plant it near the streams of heaven
Where the Son of God shines bright.

"But grow in the grace and knowledge of our Lord and Savior Jesus Christ. To him be glory both now and forever! Amen." 2 Peter 3:18 NIV

Mysteries

Mysteries of Heaven – mysteries of life,
stay ye not hidden; unburden my sight.
Open my eyes, each day just a tremor,
that I my know truth wrapped in your splendor.

My mind can't conceive – my intellect barren.
My hold on your truth is not worth comparing
to the depths of your wisdom and unveiled glory,
to visions of vastness and secrets in storage.

Unravel; release these mysteries to me;
decipher the secrets I cannot see.
Unleash and send forth on thundering wings,
ministering marvels your Spirit can bring.

Mysteries of life - mysteries of heaven,
enchanting, elusive, but why so unbidden?
Open my eyes, each day just a tremor;
delight me with wonders wrapped in God's splendor!

"The king said to Daniel, 'Surely your God is the God of gods and the Lord of kings and a revealer of mysteries, for you were able to reveal this mystery.'" Daniel 2:47 NIV

"My purpose is that they may be encouraged in heart, and united in love, so that they may have the full riches of complete understanding, in order that they may know the mystery of God, namely, Christ, in whom are hidden all the treasures of wisdom and knowledge." Colossians 2:2-3 NIV

Lord, Be There

For the battered, raped,
Incested ones
For the angry, hurt,
Defensive ones,
For the guilty, tortured,
Depressed ones,
Lord, be there.

For the lonely, lost,
Rejected ones,
For the pushed aside,
Neglected ones,
For the struggling,
Misdirected ones,
Lord, be there.

For the traumatized,
The victimized,
The prisoners of fear,
For every hurting child of yours,
Lord, be there.

"About midnight Paul and Silas were praying and singing hymns to God....Suddenly there was such a violent earthquake that the foundations of the prison were shaken. At once all the prison doors flew open, and everyone's chains came loose."
Acts 16:25:26 NIV

Adrift

We're burdened for our sons, Lord,
these precious gifts from you.
They have gone adrift Lord;
we are helpless to undo.

Rock their boats and set their sails;
and send your Wind to blow.
Chart their destination, Lord,
and teach them how to row.

Shake the decks and wake from sleep,
steady ropes and wheel.
Oh, Thou Master of the sea,
raise mast upon the keel.

When mighty waves and threatening storms
bring doubts and untold fear;
please walk upon the waters Lord;
speak loudly so they hear.

Tell them of the dangers, Lord,
adrift and so alone;
Steer them to the beaconing shore,
Their destination: home.

Light a fire upon the shore
and gather each one close.
Speak to them of truth and peace;
impart the Holy Ghost.

Empower them to live their lives
surrendered to your will;
claim these sons of ours, dear Lord,
make their spirits thrill.

Repair their boats to sail with you
to places yet unknown.

Prepare their hearts to journey on
and bring them safely home.

"Great is Thy faithfulness," O God my Father,
There is no shadow of turning in Thee;
Thou changest not, Thy compassions, they fail not:
As Thou hast been Thou forever will be.

Written by Thomas Chisholm, composed by William M. Runyan

Make Me a Light

Make me a light in the darkness, Lord;
make me a beacon to shine.
Send me on rays of the morning sun;
send me in rhythm and rhyme.

Stir up your Spirit to serve, Lord;
stir up your baptism of fire.
Light me with torches of wisdom;
equip me with all I require.

Burden my heart for souls, Lord;
bury my longings in prayer.
Wing me to struggling, oppressed ones;
wind me in ribbons to share.

Steady my heart and my footsteps;
station my will next to thine.
Sanctify, Lord, in due season;
scatter my seeds near the Vine.

"Christ himself gave the apostles, the prophets, the evangelists, the pastors and teachers to equip his people for works of service, so that the body of Christ may be built up." Ephesians 4:11-12 NIV

Wideness in Your Mercy

Loose the chains that bind, Lord;
restore this child of yours.
Give back to her a smile, Lord;
stretch it from shore to shore.

Like wideness in your mercy;
let her know your healing grace.
Renew salvation's joy, Lord;
gift her with sustaining faith.

Restore her hope in Jesus;
reestablish, intercede.
Thank You Lord for mercy,
for attending every need.

Shower her with favor,
and everlasting love.
Lavish with Your promises;
smoothing out the rough.

Give her peace for pain, Lord;
give her joy for sorrow.
Give her hope beyond belief,
and give her grace to follow.

"There's a wideness in God's mercy like the wideness of the sea.
There's a kindness in his justice which is more than liberty.
There is no place where earth's sorrows are more felt than up in heav'n.
There is no place where earth's failings have such kindly judgment giv'n.

--Hymn: "There's a Wideness in God's Mercy" Text: Fedrick W. Faber, Tune: Early American

Life is a Prayer

My whole life is praying one prayer without end.
When this life is over, I'll sing the Amen!
Each moment, each hour, each day of the week,
I look to the Lord and his guidance I seek.

Though failing and faltering, he turns not away,
forgiving, forgetting my sins of each day.
I seek him at dawning, my heart is attune;
the need he's supplying lasts barely 'til noon.

At noontime I'm crying again to my Lord.
Oh God, how I'm needing my spirit restored.
He's faithful to hear me; he knows of my need.
By evening I'm empty of all I've received.

Before I retire from the cares of each day,
Sleep won't come 'til I kneel and I pray.
I'll go on praying my prayer without end;
When life is over, I'll shout the Amen!

"Pray without ceasing." 1 Thessalonians 5:17 ESV

"I will pray morning, noon and night, pleading aloud with God, and he will hear and answer." Psalms 55:17 LB (paraphrased)

Why, Lord ?

I said, "Why, Lord?"
He said, "Why not?"
I said, "How much longer?"
He said, "Trust me."
I said, "It's lonely, Lord."
He said, "Remember Gethsemane?"

I said, "Help me!"
He said, "I'm here."
I said, "The way is dark."
He said, "I'll help you see."
I said, "How can You, Lord?"
He said, "Remember Calvary?"

I said, "I can't make it, Lord."
He said, "Rest awhile."
I said, "I'm getting weaker."
He said, "I'll strengthen soon."
I said, "Will I rise again?"
He said, "Was there an empty tomb?"

"I consider that our present sufferings are not worth comparing to the glory that will be revealed in us. For the creation waits in eager expectation for the children of God to be revealed." Romans 8:18-19 NIV

Tender My Heart

Tender my heart, Lord;
Quicken its pace.
Soften my spirit;
Render your grace.

Passion my purpose;
Gentle my mind.
Stir up your Spirit;
Loosen and bind.

Cushion my footsteps;
Lighten my load.
Softly Lord lead me;
Softly I go.

"If you have any encouragement from being united with Christ, if any comfort from his love, if any fellowship with the Spirit, if any tenderness and compassion, then make my joy complete by being like-minded, having the same love, being one in spirit and purpose." Philippians 2:1-2 NIV

Pound Him with Your Spirit

Pound him with your Spirit, Lord,
Until his very cells awaken to your truth.

Rub the oil of faith into his pores.
Knead with holy-knuckled peace.

Soothe the soreness of his soul away.
Wipe the residue so long ignored.

Towel him with righteousness and hope,
Eternity forever in his sight.

Pat him dry with sacrificial hands,
A creature new and worthy, justified.

"Jesus answered, 'I am the way, and the truth and the life. No one comes to the Father except through me.'" John 14:6 NIV

"Whoever acknowledges me before others, I will also acknowledge before my Father in heaven. But whoever disowns me before others, I will disown before my Father in heaven." Matthew 10:32-33 NIV

Holy Words

Thank you God for holy words
that stun, examine, mystify,
enrich and understand
our troubling lives.

Thank you God for holy words
that stir, convict, terrify,
reproach and reprimand
our sinful lives.

Thank you God for holy words
that fill, instill, intensify,
embrace and expand
our empty lives.

Thank You Thou, Oh Holy One,
Thou Spinner of the Psalms,
who understands without demands
our hungry, thirsting lives.

Sing them over again to me, wonderful words of life.
Let me more of thy beauty see, wonderful words of life.

Sweetly echo the gospel call, wonderful words of life.
Offer pardon and peace to all, wonderful words of life.

Jesus, only Savior, sanctify forever, wonderful words of life.
Beautiful words, wonderful words, wonderful words of life.

Hymn, "Wonderful Words of Life," Text & Tune: Philip P. Bliss

Lord, Release Me

I look out on branches heavy with snow
from last night's storm.
Even the wind does not shake them free
of this oppressive winter burden.

So like the sinking of my soul,
this bondage of body and spirit,
weighty,
exhaustive, ineffective,
subdued by passivity and pain.

Oh, God of the universe,
rescue me from this ponderous prison,
this impotence of will,
this laboring spirit.

Burn the brightness of your Son within my limbs;
melt the frigid deposits that hinder.
Free my branches
to lift and move freely again.

"…The Lord knows how to rescue the Godly from trials…" 2 Peter 2:9a NIV

"And they cried out to the Lord in their trouble, and he delivered them from their distress." Psalms 107:6 NIV

Purify

Father God,
hear my heart's cry,
Purify!

cleanse my chambers;
wash white my soul.
sanitize my spirit;
make me whole.

disinfect my mind
of thoughts impure,
tainted, unsainted,
lend your cure.

cleanse me of contamination;
rinse me in regeneration.
Father, God,
hear my heart's cry, purify!
Purify!

"Therefore, since we have these promises, dear friends, let us purify ourselves from everything that contaminates body and spirit, perfecting holiness out of reverence for God." 2 Corinthians 7:1 NIV

"Create in me a pure heart, and renew a steadfast spirit within me. Do not cast me from your presence or take the Holy Spirit from me. Restore to me the joy of my salvation and grant me a willing spirit, to sustain me." Psalms 51:10-12 NIV

Whisper Your Words

Whisper your words to me, when first I greet the morn.
Store them deep in chambers wide, with roots of Spirit-born.
Softly speak to guide my way, with holy inspiration.
Engage me with your promises; wrap me in salvation.

Be the voice within me that captures heart and mind.
Articulate, illuminate; your law and grace align.
Breathe into me O breath of God, your moral just commands;
Whisper quiet confidence into my serving hands.

Quiet fear, and reassure by faith and not by reason;
Murmur to my trembling heart, both in and out of season.
Hush conflicting voices and free me to obey;
Commit to memory all the words that you've disclosed this day.

Hide not your whispers in my heart, make me ever bold
to shout from every rooftop, to feed each struggling soul.
Bind them to my being Lord, your heavenly decree;
Remind me often of your love, and how you've set me free.

"What I tell you in the dark, speak in the daylight; what is whispered in your ear, proclaim from the roofs." Matthew 10:27 *NIV*

Hot or Cold

He'd rather I be hot or cold,
never in between,
wants my spirit to grow bold,
wants my witness seen.

Lukewarm he vows to spew me out,
cast me away from him.
If I can't love like burning coals,
how can I make amends?

He wants my temperature to rise,
my faith to be on fire,
witness always brave and bold,
be all that zeal requires.

Hand to me your Spirit torch;
light me blazing blue.
Promise you won't spew me out;
keep me on fire for you.

Determined, I will tend the fire,
that it may never die.
I want my witness strong and bold
so sparks may fly on high!

"I know your deeds, that you are neither hot nor cold. I wish you were either one or the other! So, because you are lukewarm—neither hot nor cold—I am about to spit you out of my mouth." Revelation 3:15-16 NIV

"Get on fire for God and men will come and watch you burn." --John Wesley

Puzzled Pieces Prayer

Turn the crooked pieces of my life;
make a puzzle pleasing to your eyes.
Let them fit a Godly, ordained pattern;
hear my anxious puzzled cries!

Place the sorrow where you want it;
turn the pain and make it fit.
Remove the anxious troubled pieces,
that only make me want to quit.

Creator God of priestly puzzles,
spend some mercy on this scene.
Rework my tired efforts quickly,
that I may watch you change, redeem.

Jagged pieces, sins forgiven,
replace them all with sterner stuff.
Straight and even, love constructed,
smooth those pieces that were rough.

Take the doubts and darker hues;
connect, transform them into light.
Spin the brighter pieces broadly;
make them holy in your sight.

Surrender I my broken pieces,
Let them reflect my glad rebirth,
so I may knowingly experience
a resurrected life on earth.

"We all encounter things that may seem dim and puzzling at first, but when we actively explore them, we find bold, undauntable light igniting the way from the inside, from within." —Author unknown

Splinters of Deceit

Search me, Oh Lord,
for the subtle splinters of deceit in my soul,
agents of friction, infection and dis-ease.
Tweeze them.
Squeeze them
in the fat fingers of your grace.
Let the soreness linger
that I might remember.
Amen!

> "Never be afraid to trust an unknown future to a known God."
> — Corrie ten Boom
> Trust in the Lord

"Search me, God, and know my heart; test me and know my anxious thoughts. See if there is any offensive way in me, and lead me in the way ever-lasting." Psalms 139:23-24 NIV

"Tremble and do not sin; when you are on your beds, search your hearts and be silent. Offer the sacrifices of the righteous and trust in the Lord." Psalms 4:4-5 NIV

Appointing My Days

Teach me to appoint my days,
to number each one due,
so limited in scope they are;
I would live them all for you.

Preparation is the secret;
prayer, your chosen tool.
I will pray for distant days;
commit them to your rule.

I will appoint each future day,
my eyes have not yet seen;
I will purpose them for heaven;
accept them, fat or lean.

I pray they will be vessels
of blessing and of life.
I lift up all of them to you,
release them to your light.

"Teach us to number our days and recognize how few they are; help us to spend them as we should." Psalms 92:12 LB (paraphrased)

"Surely there is a future, and your hope will not be cut off." Proverbs 23:18 RSV

Treasures

Why, Lord, do I desire things without eternal value,
things that do not bring me closer to you,
things that can be lost, stolen, or destroyed,
things that only satisfy for a season?
Why Lord?

Why do I not day by day and moment by moment
seek the things that are above,
things that quicken my spirit,
things that wrap me in wonder, love and praise,
things that cry out the kingdom of heaven,
things that create intimacy with you?
Why Lord?

Change my focus, Lord.
Redirect the longings of my heart.
Change the patterns of my life.
Reinstate the joy of your salvation.
Honor me with your presence, Lord.
I want the treasures of my heart to be eternal,
and may there be no earthly hindrance to block my way.

"I do not understand what I do. For what I want to do, I do not do, but what I hate to do. And if I do what I do not want to do, I agree that the law is good. As it is, it is no longer I myself who do it, but it is the sin living in me. For I know that good itself does not dwell in me, that is, in my sinful nature. For I have the desire to do good, but I cannot carry it out....What a wretched man I am! Who will rescue me from this body that is subject to death? Thanks be to God, who delivers me through Jesus Christ our Lord!" Romans 7:15-18, 24-25NIV

Praising Pigeons

Pigeons love to congregate high in the belfries of old churches. Is it so hard, then, to imagine that their soft coo-coo-cooing might be the offering of praises unto God? Maybe they join the ranks of the angelic beings and put forth a stirring rendition of praise and glory to their Creator. I like to think I can hear them in the early morning stillness. All breeds and species are welcome. Shake loose your feathers and flap your wings; sing praises to the Lord God Almighty!

As Christians, we are great at bringing our problems and difficulties to God. This is great, as this is exactly what God tells us to do. But, what about giving him honor, glory and praise for who he is? The Scriptures remind us that God inhabits the praises of his people. There are 112 references to praise in my NIV concordance. It must be important! God lives for our praises! Not just in church, but also in our quiet times with God, and when surrounded by his splendid creation. Christians, rise up like the pigeons and give God praise!

Upon my Altar of Praise

Upon my altar of praise,
fresh linens of love I will spread,
embroidered in red,
for the blood that He shed
to wrap me in wonder and praise.

Upon my altar of praise,
a lamp eternal will flame,
extolling his name
and his crucified frame,
now risen in glory and praise.

Upon my altar of praise,
His Word is pleading with all
to answer the call
that began with the fall,
and give him all homage and praise.

"Therefore, I urge you, brothers and sisters, in view of God's mercy, to offer your bodies as a living sacrifice, holy and pleasing to God—this is your true and proper worship. Do not conform to the pattern of this world, but be ye transformed by the renewal of your mind. Then you will be able to test and approve what God's will is— his good, pleasing and perfect will." Romans 12:1-2 NIV

April Dawn

In the early dawn,
I stand alone by my window,
caught up in the mystery of life and death.
Gentle rain tenderly nourishes
budding trees
and ripening earth.

The grass is greener than yesterday,
and plum blossoms,
which yesterday were only a promise,
are today an amazing fulfillment.

The rain falls harder than my tears,
screaming tears of anger
at the wretchedness of death,
and sadness for a loss I cannot measure.
Yet there are matching tears of joy
for the promise of life eternal.

For I am certain that in death, as in life, my friend,
you will flourish like the grass,
and blossom as the plum tree,
all the while shouting praises to God,
for your April dawn.

"Who shall separate us from the love of Christ? Shall trouble or hardship or persecution or famine or nakedness, or danger or sword?...No, in all these things we are more than conquerors through him who loved us. I am convinced that neither death nor life, neither angels nor demons, neither the present nor the future, nor any powers, neither height nor depth, nor anything else in all creation, will be able to separate us from the love of God that is in Christ Jesus." Romans 8:37-39 NIV

Morning Prayer

Grow my faith.
Unleash my love.

Let me trust
unburdened and unbent
by earthly woes.

Stretch my praises;
set no limits;
Clap my hands
to wake the morn.

Bind me in creation's glory,
eyes to see unhindered,
ears to hear your story
on this virgin day.
Whisper to the wind
to begin the matinee.

"Let the rivers clap their hands..." Psalms 98:8a NIV

"and all the trees of the field will clap their hands..." Isaiah 55:12b NIV

Suffering into Praise

Give God your groans of grief,
your inner spirit's strife,
unspoken strains beneath
the wintering of your life.

Give him the inarticulate,
the low sustaining moans,
the gravel of ill-gotten fate,
the needy spirit's drone.

Let God decipher, him translate.
Let him transform, alleviate,
turn suffering into praise,
the groans, to heaven's gaze.

"Why my soul are you downcast? Why so disturbed within me? Put your hope in God, for I will yet praise him, my Savior and my God." Psalms 42:5 NIV

"Through Jesus, therefore, let us continually offer to God a sacrifice of praise..." Hebrews 13:15a NIV

Oh, My Jesus, I Love You

Oh, my Jesus, I love you; I know in my heart you are mine.
I love your power and your glory; I love your kingdom divine.
I love your sweet gentle Spirit; I love the mercy you've shown.
I love the peace you have purchased, such peace I never have known.

I cherish each moment together; I cling to the hope that is thine.
I clutch ever tightly each promise; I claim every need that is mine.
I reach out in love to my Savior; I render a heart full of praise.
I reap a harvest of blessing; repenting, partake of your grace.

I love your light in the darkness; I love your strength when I'm weak.
I love your comfort in sorrow; I love the assurance you speak.
Oh, my Jesus I love you; I know in my heart you are mine.
I love your power and your glory; I love your kingdom divine.

"Do not be afraid, little flock, for your Father has been pleased to give you the kingdom." Luke 12:32 NIV

"Therefore since we are receiving a kingdom that cannot be shaken, let us be thankful, and so worship God acceptably with reverence and awe." Hebrews 12:28 NIV

I Found My Joy in Jesus

I found my joy in Jesus; it shall never fade away.
I find that it increases as I trust in him each day.
It's a blessing straight from heaven; joy unspeakable it is.
It will never leave me; God owns me, I am his.

I've shed some tears in sorrow; I have experienced pain.
I suffered just a little while, when trusting in his name.
At times I've been distracted; at times I've gone astray.
When I sought the Lord above, I found his better way.

I've experienced his compassion, his understanding, too.
The hurt was never greater than God's power to see me through.
I've failed God and I've fallen; I've walked and lived in sin.
But praise God, he's redeemed me,
and my joy's complete in him!

"I have told you this that my joy may be in you, and that your joy may be complete." John 15:11 NIV

"…Do not grieve, for the joy of the Lord is your strength…" Nehemiah 8:10b NIV

Showers of Blessings

Showers of blessing you promised,
right from the start of my day.
I'm wading in showers from heaven,
wet with his words on my way.

Dripping with heavenly moisture,
(I left my umbrella at home)
Bring on your showers of blessing,
Make patterns on cobblestone.

We'll sing in the precipitation;
stinging with rain from on high.
Open your windows of blessings;
I'm wonderfully wet as I sigh.

Shower, empower, embrace me;
together we splash in your name.
Father, the Son, and the Spirit,
skipping with joy in the rain.

"I will make them and the places surrounding my hill a blessing. I will send down showers in season; there will be showers of blessing. The trees will yield their fruit and the ground will yield its crops; the people will be secure in their land."
Ezekiel 34:26-27a NIV

His Rain

Rugged branches toss and bend
as if exclaiming loud "Amens."
"It is so," the wind exclaims,
then from on high, torrential rain.

Driving rain your Spirit pours,
as lively branches bend and soar.
Branches drop like bending knees,
then lift in praises up to thee.

The Spirit whispers, "Do you hear?
Does the wind and rain make clear
intention his to persevere?
His storm is not for you to fear."

"…for he makes his sun rise on the evil and on the good and sends rain on the just and the unjust…" Matt. 5:45b NIV

I Am the One

I am the One
Who leads you to green pastures to rest.
I am the One
Who removes weight from your heart and your soul.
Yes, I am the One.

I am the One
Who breathes new life into you.
I am the One
Who makes you, again, like new.
Yes, I am the One.

I am the One
Who speaks softly his Word.
I am the One
Who carries when you cannot walk.
Yes, I am the One.

I am the One
Who bids you to eat and to drink.
I am the One
Who anoints you with oil.
Yes, I am the One.

I am the One
Who meets you by quiet waters.
I am the One
Who causes your cup to overflow.
Yes, I am the One,
And I am here!

"*The Lord is my shepherd, I shall not be in want.*" Psalm 23:1 NIV

"*I am the Lord, and there is no other; apart from me there is no God. I will strengthen you.*" Isaiah 45:5a NIV

Holy Be His Name

My Father in heaven, holy be your name;
yesterday and forever,
You remain the same.

When I lift my praises, I call you Abba, Father;
surrounded by your angels,
worshipped like none other.

I am deep in holiness, perfect Son of God,
most perfect friend I'll ever have;
I am the one who's flawed.

Alpha and Omega, beginning and the end,
You gladly make a way for me,
and every flaw You mend.

Holy, holy God, unto You I raise
Myself to be your dwelling;
I'm lost in love and praise.

"Holy, holy, holy! All the saints adore thee,
casting down their golden crowns around the glassy sea.
Cherubim and seraphim falling down before thee,
which wert and art and evermore shall be."

Hymn: Holy, Holy, Holy, Text: Reginald Heber, Tune: K. Strassbur

A Crown in Heaven

My heart and spirit sing as I praise the King of Kings,
    never seeking worldly wealth or men's reward.
When this life is past, only work for Christ will last,
    and I'll wear a crown in heaven from my Lord.

I seek not earthly fame; only choose to praise his name.
    My allegiance is to Christ and not to men.
As I look to him above, God of grace and God of love;
    I long to labor for his kingdom without end.

Though my light my never be ever bright that all may see,
    I humbly pray my dim-lit light may shine.
As God lives within my heart, may I faithfully impart
    his kingdom's life and love which He designed.

Yes, my inward spirit sings praises to the King of Kings,
    serving him on earth is great reward.
I know no greater joy than to be in his employ,
    looking forward to the harvest of the Lord!

"Do you not know that in a race all the runners run, but only one gets the prize? Run in such a way as to get the prize….we do it to get a crown that will last forever." 1 Corinthians 9:24-25 NIV

"Let us not become weary in doing good, for at the proper time we will reap a harvest if we don't give up." Galatians 6:9 NIV

Shout Hallelujah!

I found the Lord! No, the Lord found me!
I'm in the Lord! No, the Lord's in me!
I said I'm sorry, and I turned from sin;
He took my hand and I followed him.

Shout Hallelujah! Sing the Amen!
Praise to the Lord I am saved from sin!
He is my Father; I am his child.
His Holy Spirit on me has smiled.

He changed my life; I was born again.
He took my hand and I followed him.
Sing hallelujah! Shout the Amen!
Jesus my Lord is coming again!

"Jesus replied, 'with all the earnestness I possess, I tell you this: Unless you are born again, you can never get into the Kingdom of God.'" John 3:3 LB (paraphrased)

"Jesus called a small child over to him and set the little fellow down among them and said, 'Unless you turn to God from your sins and become as little children, you will never get into the Kingdom of Heaven. Therefore, anyone who humbles himself as this little child, is the greatest in the Kingdom of Heaven.' "
Matthew 18:2-3 LB (paraphrased)

Rejoice in the Lord

This is the day that the Lord has made;
let us rejoice and be glad.
The heavens are open; his love has been spoken;
there is no cause to be sad.

Shout for the joy in your soul;
clap for his grace over you.
Dance before him who covers all sin;
delight that he makes all things new.

Celebrate his glory and power,
rejoice in the blessings he gives.
His joy is my strength; his timing in sync;
I'll praise him as long as I live.

"Therefore we do not lose heart. Though outwardly we are wasting away, yet inwardly we are being renewed day by day. For our light and momentary troubles are achieving for us an eternal glory that far outweighs them all. For we fix our eyes not on what is seen, but on what is unseen, since what is seen is temporary, but what is unseen is eternal. 2 Corinthians 4:16-18 NIV

"Better is one day in your courts than a thousand days elsewhere." Proverbs 84:10 NIV

The Dance

The trees and the wind are partners,
today, stepping high on their ride;
Bouncing in tune with the branches,
dancing their polka in stride.

Lifting their limbs in the twilight,
driven like waves on the sea;
Spreading their wild celebration
up to my window, and me.

Then ever so quickly, they falter,
both take deep breaths and exhale.
The wind returns, then, and is ready,
Parading his white tie and tail.

They lift and they dip like the surfers,
keeping their balance in check;
Winding through leaves in the fox trot,
and NOW, for the fifth inning stretch.

They turn to each other with purpose,
lifting their branches toward heaven;
Praising their God and Creator,
for the mighty dance he has given.

"Let the fields be jubilant, and everything in them; let all the trees of the forest sing (dance) for joy." Psalms 96:12 NIV (paraphrase mine)

Fantail Pigeons

These flashy birds are probably the most recognizable and well-known of the fancy pigeons. Their peacock-like tails, prominent chests, and curved necks are a hit in bird shows and fairground livestock shows around the world. They serve more purpose than just flashiness, though. Racing or homing pigeon breeders often keep fantails at the front of the loft landing while they are training their new prospects. The highly-visible fantails guide the young ones home like a beacon. **(Excerpts from Wikipedia Commons)**
One might say that fantails are full of beauty and grace.

Fantails are flashy – so is our God! He stretched forth his hand and created the world. We only have to focus our eyes on his rainbow in the sky to remind us of the beauty of his creation. His grace is evident every day as he pours out grace upon grace, and he sends his Holy Spirit like a heavenly beacon, not just to train the young, but to guide and empower us in every stage of our Christian journey. Flashy? You bet! Full of beauty and grace.

Ella

What is that, Grandma?
Why, it's a needle made of steel.
Oh, Grandma, can I feel?

What is that, Grandma?
Why, it's thread that I clutch.
Oh, Grandma, can I touch?

What do you sew, Grandma?
Why, a soft quilt for my bed.
Oh, Grandma, can you lay it by my head?

Little fingers, curiously,
Reach out to touch and feel
Textures soft, sharp, and smooth –
Then a big grin – and a squeal!

"Work hard and cheerfully at all that you do, just as though you were working for the Lord…" Colossians 3:23a LB (paraphrased)

Emma

I stood nearby as she carefully climbed
to the top step of the ladder.
ornaments in hand,
she reached and stretched
as if on a dare,
perfectly placing them
near the very top of the tree,
the shiny splendor
matching her golden hair.

As I watched,
somehow I knew
she would always be reaching
and stretching further than most,
balancing precariously
on the top shelf of life,
as if on a dare,
this independent girl,
Emma, with the golden hair.

"Trust in the Lord and do good…Take delight in the Lord and he will give you the desires of your heart." Psalms 37:3a, 4 NIV

Living Waters

Linger at the fountain of God's favor;
quench your thirst in rivers of his love.
Satisfy your soul in saving water;
you will drink, but never get enough.

Hold your breath while visions overtake you,
wonders of his world to contemplate.
Enjoy the stillness of the living waters,
drop your anchor deep and meditate.

"and if you look for it as for silver and search for it as hidden treasure, you will understand the fear of the Lord and find the knowledge of God." Proverbs 2:4 NIV

"Oh, the depth of the riches of the wisdom and the knowledge of God! How unsearchable his judgments, and his paths beyond tracing out." Romans 11:33 NIV

Rainbow Grace

He stirs his grace abundant,
he spreads it thick like honey;
colors it like a rainbow,
on dark days or the sunny.

He showers us with blessings
of every shape and size.
Some are most apparent,
others in disguise.

He gives us words of wisdom,
and proverbs to translate.
His miracles of language,
he helps us navigate.

Don't take one day for granted;
never fail to recognize
the colors in his rainbow
or the grace that he supplies.

"I have set my rainbow in the clouds, and it will be the sign of the covenant between me and the earth…Never again will the waters become a flood to destroy all life." Genesis 9:13,15b NIV

"At once I was in the Spirit, and there before me was a throne in heaven with someone sitting on it. And the one who sat there had the appearance of jasper and ruby. A rainbow that shone like an emerald encircled the throne." Revelation 4:2-3 NIV

Son, Are You Ready to Fly?

The years have passed quickly, son;
it seems like only yesterday
you were received by God in Holy Baptism.

You were a tiny, precious bundle,
a human cocoon,
wrapped in your yellow thermo blanket,
eyes exploring your curious new world;
busy limbs throwing off your covers,
an infant butterfly stirring with new life.

God's grace has allowed you to wiggle free
of your thermo nest,
grow beyond its boundaries,
wobbly adventurous legs
strengthened in your journey.

Today, my son, God's Spirit calls you
to a new challenge.
He would have you fly!
Are you anxious to soar, to explore
new dimensions in the Spirit?
Are you prepared to let
God determine your flight patterns?
Can you submit to the disciplines of flying?
Are you ready to affirm your wings of faith?

If so, say "I do,
and I ask God to help and guide me." *

"But you will receive power when the Holy Spirit comes on you, and you will be my witnesses in Jerusalem, and in all Judea and Samaria, and to the ends of the earth." Acts 1:8 NIV

*Tim's Confirmation, May 1981

Galaxy of Grace

Grabbed by grace one awesome day,
washed in tears of shame.
God caught my tears and calmed my fears;
he boldly called my name.

Seized by grace, he set my feet
on higher, holy ground.
He clasped my hand, helped me to stand;
he turned my life around.

Empowered by grace, I followed him,
set sights on things above.
Aroused by faith, I ventured forth,
delighting in his love.

Saving grace, you rescued me;
one day I'll see your face.
Right now content, my life be spent
in your galaxy of grace.

"Oh, to grace how great a debtor, daily I'm constrained to be.
Let that grace now like a fetter bind my wand'ring heart to thee.
Jesus sought me when a stranger wand'ring from the fold of God.
He to rescue me from danger, interposed his precious blood."

Hymn: "Come Thou Fount of Every Blessing", Text, Robert Robinson, Tune, J. Wyeth

A Bible of My Own

"A Bible of my own," I heard my son exclaim,
a treasured gift, God's holy Word, imprinted with his name.
I shared in his excitement,
I sensed his inner joy;
prayed that God would activate the faith of my young boy.

That my son be stirred to service by the Spirit of the Lord,
more than just a hearer, but a doer of God's Word.
Within its holy pages
he'd lose his life, but gain his soul,
learn life begins with dying if one would be made whole.

I prayed this Bible of his own would never gather dust,
that faith would be his fortune and God would be his trust.
Give hope when he's down-hearted,
grace sufficient for his day,
wisdom for life's troubles, God's love to light the way.

That as he grew to manhood, he would also grow in grace;
as he grew in wisdom, God's Word would have a place.
Though on this day, my son, you boast,
"A Bible of my own,"
I pray that you will use it to make God's kingdom known.

"For the word of God is alive and active, sharper than any double-edged sword, it penetrates even to dividing soul and spirit, joints and marrow; it judges the thoughts and attitudes of the heart. Nothing in all creation is hidden from God's sight. Everything is uncovered and laid bare before the eyes of him to whom we must give account." Hebrews 4:12-13 NIV

Jody

"Happiness makes up in height
for what it lacks in length,"
an epitaph well-chosen for this child.
I read the words again, and forced a smile.

He was only ten, small for his age,
but stretched against adversity,
he looked tall, remarkably tall.

He didn't speak German or French, Latin or Greek.
His language was rooted in love,
structured with pain.

He built his vocabulary on challenge,
mastered the semantics of suffering,
and spent his lifetime in conversation with courage.

A child prodigy tutored by Leukemia,
he patiently instructed us in higher mathematics,
teaching us to add gratefully, subtract willingly,
upsetting the tables of multiplication.

Jody proved
that pain, multiplied by faith, equals joy,
and that a full life is not measured
in days, months or years,
but rather in cups, pints and quarts.

"Where, O death, is your victory, where, O death is your sting?"
1 Corinthians 15:5 NIV

"...but it has now been revealed through the appearing of our Savior, Christ Jesus, who has destroyed death and has brought life and immortality to light through the gospel." 2 Timothy 1:10 NIV

Quiet Times

I thank you God for quiet times,
the Spirit's in between,
to turn a page,
to hold a thought,
to shed a tear unseen.

To gain perspective on my life,
prioritize anew,
to reaffirm there is no life
apart from loving you.

I thank you God for quiet times
behind closed chamber doors,
where peace and pain
join hands in dance,
while grace on grace is poured.

"*...in quietness and trust is your strength...*" Isaiah 30:15b NIV

"*I needed the quiet so He drew me aside, into the shadows where we could confide. Away from the bustle where all the day long, I hurried and worried when active and strong. I needed the quiet, no prison my bed, but a beautiful valley of blessings instead. A place to grow richer, in Jesus to hide. I needed the quiet so He drew me aside.*"

-*Alice Hansche Mortenson*

Everlasting

Everlasting light
Illuminates my way
Beacon never failing
Radiant day by day

Lamp upon my feet
Everlasting glow
Rays of golden sunlight
You on me bestow

Everlasting promises
Solid saving Words
Treasures of the Kingdom
Double-edged swords

Passages of peace and joy
Psalms of endless praise
Warnings penned by prophets
Chapters filled with grace

Everlasting love for me
The sacrificial cross
The blessed Holy Spirit
Salvation for the lost

Everlasting promises
Everlasting light
Everlasting love of God
Knows no depth nor height

"Before the mountains were born or you brought forth the whole world, from everlasting to everlasting you are God. Psalms 90:2 NIV

Signature of Heaven

The signature of heaven
Is before me;
The letter of His love
Is deep within.
The message of the Cross
In blood is written,
The essence of a world saved from sin.

I behold God's signature,
His grace
and saving cure;
I hold His letter high that I might see.
I clutch it boldly in my hand;
Send it forth to every land,
His salutation isn't just for me.

The signature of heaven
Seals the story
Of how our Savior, Jesus,
Came from glory.
This epistle dipped in blood
Will always be enough
To steal and seal our hearts with His love.

"He said to them, 'Go into all the world and preach the gospel to all creation.'"
Mark 16:15 NIV

Music of Heaven

I want the music of heaven to come down.
I want the symphony of angels to abound.
Hit the high notes and the low,
For blessed harmony below;
Spread the music of your heavens all around.

Prompt my heavy heart to sing
With gratitude in everything.
String the harp and send it down;
In the arms of heaven's clowns.
Give me joy, blessed joy, in suffering.

Let me dance amid your grace
And behold you face to face.
Oh, let the trumpet sound;
Beat the drums uphill and down.
Let me your love and comfort taste.

Your bells for me will sound;
They will never be too loud.
All I have I offer Thee;
More like You I wish to be.
I want the music of heaven to come down.

"Sing for joy to God our strength; shout aloud to the God of Jacob! Begin the music, strike the timbrel, play the melodious harp and lyre." Psalms 81:1-2 NIV

Let the Children Come

Quiet scooters brush the air
around my legs and feet.
Graceful little bodies
turn and twist
to silent beat.

Deep we drift in Bible study;
deep are they in play.
Holy words fly through the air,
advance the children's way.

Jesus is among us,
arms wide open flung,
whispering softly,
"Please let the children come!"

"Children are a heritage from the Lord, offspring a reward from him."
Psalms 127:3 NIV

"People were bringing little children to Jesus for him to place his hands on them. But the disciples rebuked them. When Jesus saw this, he was indignant. He said to them 'Let the little children come to me, and do not hinder them, for the kingdom of God belongs to such as these.'" Mark 10:13-15 NIV

The Pharisee and the Publican

"I thank God that I am not like other sinful men,"
the Pharisee concluded with a loud and firm **"Amen."**
He beat his breast in arrogance, and grand self-righteousness,
enumerating virtues, extolling Godliness.

**"I keep the Sabbath holy;
I pray six times a day.
I tithe of all my earthly goods;
I fast religiously."**

Another offered up his prayer; raised his eyes toward heaven.
"Be merciful to me," he said, **"a sinner, unforgiven."**
No pompous words to justify, but courage to confess,
with empty hands and heavy heart, his own unworthiness.

**I've broken every law, oh God,
yet dare to come to thee.
Forgive me Lord, I beg of you;
be merciful to me."**

"I tell you that this man (tax collector) rather than the other went home justified before God. For all those who exalt themselves will be humbled, and those who humble themselves will be exalted." Luke 18:14 NIV

Inheritance from God

I'm richer far than any man
with worldly wealth or fame.
I'm wonderfully wealthy,
for in Christ I've staked a claim.

I may never build a mansion,
but I'll always have a home;
a place prepared in heaven
that I know will be my own.

I may never know of interest drawn
from money in the bank,
but greater are the dividends
for which my God I thank.

My home won't be a show place
of earthly treasures rare;
my heart belongs in heaven
with the treasures that are there.

I may never see my name spelled out
in twinkling neon lights,
but I know that it's recorded
in the kingdom without night.

I may never see the Holy Land
or travel far and wide,
but I'll see the new Jerusalem;
with Christ I shall abide.

I may never be a wealthy heir
nor do I wish to be,
but God has left a rich and rare
inheritance for me.

Money cannot ever buy
such safe and solid ground.

Possessions cannot equal
the security I've found.

The world can never satisfy
one's spirit or his soul,
for only God can set you free,
can cleanse and make you whole.

"Do not store up for yourselves treasures on earth where moths and vermin destroy, and where thieves break in and steal. But store up for yourselves treasures in heaven...for where your treasure is, there your heart will be also."
Matthew 6:19-20a, 21 NIV

"He will be the sure foundation for your times, a rich store of salvation and wisdom and knowledge; the fear of the Lord is the key to this treasure." Isaiah 33:6 NIV

Abba, Father, God!

Lord, turn the hearts of stone
Into hearts of flesh!
Let them by the Spirit cry
"Abba, Father, God!"
Release the Spirit's power,
Let their lips confess
Offering heavy sin
To Abba, Father, God!

Let them eat your living Words
Feel the Spirit grow.
Reveal yourself to them
As Abba, Father, God!
Let them walk redeemed,
And let them all say so.
SHOUT, "I've been redeemed
By Abba, Father, God!"

"Because you are his sons, God has sent the Spirit of His Son into our hearts, the Spirit who calls out 'Abba, Father,' so you are no longer a slave, but God's child...."
Galatians 6-7a NIV

Mighty Magnet

Like a mighty magnet, the Holy Spirit draws
on rushing winds beneath him,
providing shock and awe.
Fireworks light up the sky, his bundle of surprise;
he lights upon the newest,
with fire in his eyes.

Excelling and indwelling the searching hearts of men,
approved by God the Father;
his Spirit to descend.
It falls on those he chooses, apples of his eye,
just waiting for his Spirit;
he's heard their eager cries.

Like a mighty magnet,
The Holy Spirit draws.
Rushing winds beneath him
distribute shock and awe!

"*But after me (John) comes one who is more powerful than I, whose sandals I am not worthy to carry. He will baptize you with the Holy Spirit and fire.*" *John 3:11 NIV*

"*Spirit of the Living God, fall afresh on me.*
Spirit of the Living God, fall afresh on me.
Melt me, mold me, fill me, use me.
Spirit of the living God, fall afresh on me."

Hymn: "Spirit of the Living God", C. Michael Hawn

Lily Pads on Loon Lake

I dangled my feet from the dock
while lily pads bobbed
in shallow water.

Like shiny green sand dollars
gently floating,
freely suspended
invisibly rooted.

Slender arms reaching out
connecting,
embracing
their sister lilies,
lifting golden heads
like friends,
like us.

"A friend loves at all times, and a brother is born for times of adversity."
Proverbs 17:17 NIV

"Friendship is always a sweet responsibility, never an opportunity." -Kahil Gilbran

Assembly of Driftwood

like a congregation of driftwood
washed ashore in the fullness of time
we came to rest, rejoice and reminisce
no longer sprouting the green twigs of our youth
admiring our slender stems
inebriated with the fragrance
of promising buds and fragile blossoms
we are different, you and me
since we in faith put out to sea

decades of riding the waves
have stripped us of our bark
yet we are not ashamed of our nakedness

disappointments
sorrows
failures
have left us crooked
where we fancied ourselves straight
rough where we deemed ourselves smooth
brittle where we gloried in our strength

brilliant twigs have become broken logs
with twisting tunnels and widening pores
still He bids us rejoice in our brokenness
we are different, you and me
living
breathing
intimately
we are an assembly of driftwood
peering at each other through hollowed windows
and ragged doors
discovering that sanctification
is a downward ascent
we are different
you and me
living

**dying
gracefully**

"When pride comes, then comes disgrace, but with humility comes wisdom."
Proverbs 11:2 NIV

Kathleen at 99

A wisp of a woman
with loose white curls
framing a slightly wrinkled face
of librarian wisdom and inner strength.

Every day I marvel at her aged body
pursuing exercises to keep fit for yet another day
and encouraging us to do likewise.
"I need it," she says.

Lately she can be seen on the deck
with her walker
and pants rolled to her knees,
allowing the sun to bath her lower legs.
"I'm a crazy lady,"
she frequently says.
Yes, crazy in love with life
and her Creator –
We should all be that crazy.

And besides she boasts,
"still have all my own teeth!"
She has a right to be proud
of every tooth
and every year of her vibrant life!

"Is not wisdom found among the aged? Does not long life bring understanding?"
Job 12:12 NIV

"Growing old, still play the child; Keep some glory undefiled.
What if clouds are mist and air? Still see ships sailing there.
Still build castles in the air! Still see white ships sailing there!
Still have something to pursue, Something which you wish you knew."
--Edgar Guest, "Keep Your Dreams" (excerpts)

Grace

He dishes out His grace
like scoops of free ice cream.
Don't need to stand in line;
He graciously redeems.

Like a land of milk and honey,
like a mountain rising high.
We extend our hand to him;
he listens for our sigh.

We can take our time and linger;
it will never melt away.
Our ice cream runneth over
in a most delightful way.

It's flavor made in heaven,
shipped in buckets from on high,
puts a smile on every face;
it comes in great supply.

There is one condition,
then you are in the loop.
Come as often as you need to,
but you supply the scoop!

"...in order that in the coming ages he might show the incomparable riches of his grace, expressed in his kindness to us in Christ Jesus." Ephesians 2:7 NIV

Stranger-Friend

There's a stranger at my door whom I've never seen before,
but I behold a countenance of love.
From the shadows I explore, hands knocking evermore,
yet soft, like someone wearing gloves.
Coming closer I can see, He's carrying gifts addressed to me;
desire gives way to doubt and unbelief.
Even though they're labeled "free" and He says they're just for me;
I question gifts so easy to receive.

But He does not go away; He knocks throughout the day,
and the radiance of His face is like the sun.
His face does not portray impatience or dismay,
but a willingness to finish work begun.
All at once I hear Him speak, "I will knock but you must seek.
I want to give, but you must first receive."

Ever cautiously I peek, then longingly I seek,
swinging wide the door, so anxious to believe.
With increasing trust in him, I invite the stranger in,
and He became a resident that day.
I'm still unwrapping gifts; with each one my Spirit lifts,
I know my Stranger-Friend is here to stay.

"Every good and perfect gift is from above, coming down from the Father of heavenly lights, who does not change like shifting shadows." James 1:17 NIV

The Christening

Cross-legged she sat
sobbing to the cupboards,
whimpering to the kitchen floor
(a sibling quarrel and she no match for older brothers)

I left the dirty dishes and joined her sulky sit-in,
searching for words
to heal her wounded spirit,
desperate to belong,
to be someone but a tag-a-long.

Mother and daughter cross-legged,
templed in their private tee-pee,
a comic pair poised for ceremony.
"You not tag-a-long, you Little Feather;
You tickle hearts. You Somebody."

She giggled and snuggled closer,
"and you Big Feather,"
she said.

"A happy heart makes the face cheerful, but heartache crushes the spirit." Proverbs 15:13 NIV

"The first to apologize is the bravest, the first to forgive is the strongest, and the first to forget is the happiest.
—Author unknown

This I Know

I guess that I will never know
why God in heaven loves me so,
why Christ was born and chose to die
to save a sinner such as I.

I guess that I will never know
just why his blessings overflow,
or why his grace will never end,
or why he chose to be my friend.

But this I know, he does love me,
died on a Cross to set me free;
salvation only his to give;
I know because of him I live.

"Amazing grace! How sweet the sound that saved a wretch like me.
I once was lost, but now am found, was blind, but now I see.
The Lord has promised good to me, His word my hope secures.
He will my shield and portion be as long as life endures."

Hymn: Amazing Grace. John Newton

"Who can fathom the mysteries of God? Can you probe the limits of the Almighty? They are higher than the heavens above...They are deeper than the depths below...Measure is longer than the earth...wider than the sea." Job 11:7-9 NIV

Vanity

Life is not us before a mirror
Admiring features
Standing near
Extolling virtues
Make-up that glows
Reciting successes
While dabbing our nose
Blushing our cheeks
Clipping our toes
Lining our lips
In self-styled pose.

Turn from the mirror
That reflects only you
Find the real pulse
In things that you do
Render your praises
To whom they belong
Give God the glory
Start singing His song.

"*Vanity of vanities, says the Preacher, vanity of vanities! All is vanities!* Ecclesiastes 1:2-3 RSV

"*Charm is deceitful, and beauty is vain, but a woman who fears the Lord is to be praised.*" Proverbs 31:30 RSV

Pulpit Pigeons

Pulpit Pigeons deliver sermons, acting always on a higher authority. Their pulpits may be high in a church belfry or barn, a cleft of rocks, or a high-rise building. They perch wherever they can find an open space. In lieu of a robe or cowl, they wear a suit of feathers of various colors. They preach to whomever will listen, bird or man, woman or child, beast or fowl. If you have ears to hear, listen!

As Christians, we can preach sermons in one word or many. We are advised to preach the Word "in season" and "out," good times and bad. God has promised to supply us with the words we need at the time we need them. No need to be anxious about what we will say. No need for fear. We can deliver our messages to one person or many. Sermons can be given, or heard in churches, parks, houses, ships, back-yards, or wherever the Spirit (or pigeon) "nudges" you. If you have ears to hear, listen.

Can't Take it with You

You'll never see a hearse
with a luggage rack;*
You'll never see a grave
lined with gold.
You will leave this earth
with nothing on your back,
no jewels that enslave;
can't trust their anchor-hold.

Carry only Words of Life,
songs of hope and joy;
the resurrected Lord
will meet you there.
Walk toward the after-life
anxious to enjoy
graciously restored
by faith, a brand new billionaire.

David Rockefeller

"Do not store up for yourselves treasures on earth, where moths and vermin destroy, and where thieves break in and steal. For where your treasure is, there your heart will be also." Matthew 6:19-21

Set Your Hand to the Plow

Every farmer of the Word
So many times has heard:
Set your hand to the plow;
    Don't turn back.

Plow the straight and even rows;
Watch the love and hope that grows.
Set your hand to the plow;
    Don't turn back.

You will come on rocky ground
Where obstacles abound.
Set your hand to the plow;
    Don't turn back.

Forgetting what is past;
Only straight ahead will last.
Set your hand to the plow;
    Don't turn back.

"Jesus replied, 'No one who puts a hand to the plow and looks back is fit for service in the kingdom of God.'" Luke 9:62 NIV

Covenant God

Amazing,
Abundant
Astonishing God
Constructing
Erupting
A covenant love.

No turning
Adjourning
This wonder of heaven
Believe it
Receive it
For you it is given

Embrace it
Encase it
And lace it with might
Affirm it
Discern it
From death into life.

"The days are coming, declares the Lord, when I will make a new covenant with the people of Israel and with the people of Judah. It will not be like the covenant I made with my ancestors when I took them by the hand to lead them out of Egypt, because they did not remain faithful to my covenant, and I turned away from them, declares the Lord. This is the covenant I will establish with the people of Israel after that time, declares the Lord. I will put my laws in their minds and write them on their hearts. I will be their God, and they will be my people." Hebrews 8b, 9-10 NIV

Faithful in Small Things

I haven't preached to thousands,
Nor fed the multitudes;
I haven't gone across the sea
To spread God's wondrous news.

I have not sheltered homeless,
Or spoke of God in prisons;
I haven't learned a language new
To spread evangelism.

I've not walked with you like Peter,
I have never prayed like Paul.
I've not trusted you like Mary,
Nor like the widow, gave my all.

I am not among the scholars
Who discern your prophecy;
I am awed by Solomon's wisdom;
I am stunned by what I see.

And yet I do not envy them,
these brave ambassadors;
If I serve him well in little things,
He might just hand me more.

"*His master replied, 'Well done, good and faithful servant! You have been faithful with a few things; I will put you in charge of many things. Come and share your master's happiness.'" Matthew 25:21 NIV*

Joy Comes in the Morning

Spring is just around the corner
Around the ice and slippery slopes
Around winter's harsh and bitter strokes
Around the snow and driving winds

Around storms that isolate and sting
Around this season's darkened wreath
Around my struggling faith beneath
Spring is Just around the corner

Joy is just around the corner
Around the bleakness of my strife
Around my dark soul's bitter fight
Around the blinding storms of life

Around the darkness of my night
Around the tears that tear my heart
Around the fear that doubt imparts.
Joy is just around the corner.

Weeping is but for a night
Morning brings my soul to flight
Freezing temps give way to spring
Mounting joy that makes me sing

My heavy heart is riding high
Death and darkness to defy
Gradually my spirit's warming
Alas! Joy comes in the morning.

"His anger lasts a moment; His favor lasts for life! Weeping may go on all night, but in the morning there is joy." Psalms 30:5 NIV

"Restore to me the joy of your salvation, and grant me a willing spirit, to sustain me." Psalms 51:12 NIV

Come!

"Can any good from Nazareth come?
Nathanial asked in doubt.
"Come and see," said Philip;
Then both sought Jesus out.
"You will see the heavens open,
Angelic hosts in mass,
Ascending and descending
Upon the Son of Man.
Come!"
(John 1:45, 51 paraphrased)
+ + +
"Come see what God has done,
Awesome deeds for all mankind!
He rules! He reigns!
Calling hearts with His to bind.
Let the sounds of praise be heard
Above the clamor of the world.
With His grace our lives preserved;
Shone His light when darkness swirled.
Come!
(Psalms 66:5-6 paraphrased)
+ + +
"Come, ye blessed of my father;
Everything I have is yours.
I was hungry and you fed me,
And when in thirst, you poured.
You aided needy, oppressed souls,
Visited them in prison;
Weakened satan's bitter hold.
Grew in love and wisdom.
Come!
(Matthew 25:34-40 paraphrased)
+ + +

"Breakfast is ready, come!"
Disciples pulled their nets.
They recognized the risen Lord
Who cancelled all their debts.
"Do you love me, Simon Peter?"
(When fish and bread were gone)
Triple reassurance given,
Now waits for us to come.
Come!
(John 21:12-17 paraphrased)
\+ \+ \+
The Spirit and the Bride say "Come!"
Let those who hear say "Come!"
Call all who thirst to come!
It is finished; it is done.
Freely take, and freely give
Invitations from our God.
Share His prophecy, this scroll;
Water of Life has made you whole!
Come!
(Revelation 22:17 paraphrased)

He Knew

We didn't ask Jesus to die on the cross;
We didn't ask him to forgive us our sin.
We didn't ask him to pour out his love –
But he did.

We didn't know we needed a cross
For consequences of sin;
We didn't know we needed his love;
Only his Father did.

Would we have dared to ask for the cross
If we knew we would die in our sin?
Would we have sought unjustified love?
Crucified flesh for us?

The question is mute, hangs in the air;
Not relevant here to debate.
Christ hung there; blood everywhere,
And only the Father knew.

"…for your Father knows what you need before you ask him." Matthew 6:8b NIV

Whoever Has Ears, Listen!

It's our heart
It's our hearing
That keeps the door closed tight
He doesn't barge
He doesn't charge
He doesn't start a fight.

He just waits
At your gate
His eyes upon the door
He is patient
At his station
While you turn and pace the floor

Waiting for your ears
Hardened wax to clear
Tympanic chambers ready to receive
Ears that open wide
Hear his voice inside
Offering up your spirit to believe

"Whoever has ears, let them hear." Matthew 11:15 NIV

All is Well

Rejoice in the darkest places. Rejoice!
Know the love that makes you whole.
Know the peace that covers all.
Rejoice! Again I say, rejoice!

Know the mercy of my heart,
Loving you right from the start,
Lifting you to higher plains,
Granting blessing in my name.

I have draped you in my glory;
I have wound you in my story.
I have kept you safe, secure,
Grace of Spirit to endure.

Always present,
Always leading;
Trust me now
To do thy bidding.

Rejoice! Again, I say, rejoice!
Watch my Spirit leap and swell.
Lean on me, child,
All is well.

"They will be my people and I will be their God. I will give them singleness of heart and action, so that they will always fear me and that all will go well for them and for their children after them." Jeremiah 32:39 NIV

Jubilee!

This is the day of your salvation;
    this is the year of Jubilee.*
When the prophets of Israel thundered
    messages God had decreed.

Elijah declared the Word of the Lord,
    days of great trials on earth.
Moses heard God, answered his call;
    righteousness needed rebirth.

Ezekiel had his day in the sun,
    dry bones becoming as flesh.
The dead were spoken to life again
    with just a few words, and a breath.

David rebuilt a temple for praise
    with a heart that sought after God;
singing his songs and playing the harp,
    he worshipped in wonder and awe.

Later, a voice in the wilderness cried,
    "Prepare ye the way of the Lord."
Make your paths straight; repent of your sins;
    experience your spirit restored.

The Israelites had their own Jubilee
    after fifty long years had passed,
A time to rejoice and cancel all debts;
    this was a gift unsurpassed.

A day full of grace, slaves were set free,
    and property justly returned.
Half a century of counting each day,
    a Jubilee for which their hearts burned.

Our Jubilee came with Jesus the Christ,
dying to set all men free.
Our bondage was sin; our consequence, death.
His Spirit our apt referee.

Christ canceled our debts, future and past;
of his Kingdom we're heirs.
Today let it be your grand Jubilee;
Don't wait for 50 more years!

"In the year of Jubilee the field shall return to the one from whom it was bought…"
Leviticus 27:24

*To ensure that the people would not oppress, enslave or exploit one another, or accumulate unreasonable wealth, God told Moses that every 50th year would be a year of jubilee. At this time all land would be given back to its original owner without payment, all indentured servants were to be released from their obligation, and all cultivated land was to lie fallow. Although it is unlikely that these dicta were ever carried out, the jubilee served to remind Israel that everything ultimately belonged to the Lord. "The land shall not be sold in perpetuity, for the land is mine."
Leviticus 25:23

I Was the Woman

I was the woman at the well;
a stranger came and asked me for a drink.
He told me all about my sordid past;
my head hung low, my eyes downcast.
He did not judge me nor condemn;
he treated me much like a daughter.
He said if only I desired,
he would give me Living Water.

I was the woman with adulterous past,
facing a mob armed with stone.
A stranger came, dismissed them with shame,
and offered my sins to atone.
He lifted me up from my guilt and shame,
promised his love to restore.
"You are cleansed, forgiven, my child;
go now and sin no more."

I was the woman with precious perfume,
when I met Jesus my Lord.
Though once lost in sin;
I now followed him,
and let him completely restore.

He is my teacher, Savior and friend;
I anointed his feet with my hair.
He died on a cross; my gain was his loss;.
He left ME his Gospel to share.

"Jesus straightened up and asked her, ' Woman, where are they? Has no one condemned you?' 'No one sir,' she said. 'Then neither do I condemn you,' Jesus declared. 'Go now and leave your life of sin'" John 8:10-11 NIV

Golden Glimpses

I live on golden glimpses
of God's eternal light,
rare moments in his presence
when I behold him shining bright.
Maybe it was just a word
I came to understand
at a deep and richer level;
perhaps this was your plan.

Music made in heaven,
the pathway to my soul,
spreading light upon my way;
perhaps that was your goal.
Praying, you are present
with somber streams of light.
At worship you're a beacon;
you are my shining knight.

I know they're only glimpses,
filtered rays and beams,
but I treasure every insight;
I never use sun-screen!

"For God, who said, let light shine out of darkness, made his light shine in our hearts to give us the light of the knowledge of God's glory displayed in the face of Christ."
2 Corinthians 4:6 NIV

Jesus Explosion

A child asks, "If Jesus lives in my heart,
will it explode?"
Oh, yes, my child;
your little heart
will burst with love and great joy!

It will be pulled apart at the seams,
and shower you with forgiveness
and everlasting life.

You will sparkle with faith;
you will shine like the stars.
You will make friends with Jesus
as he explodes within you
with all the colors of the rainbow!

Yes, my child,
your Jesus heart will explode,
and you will glimpse
the beauty of God's Kingdom.

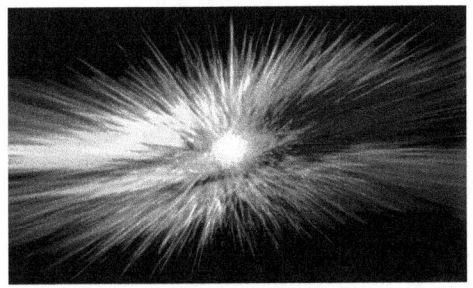

"Jesus loves me! He who died, Heaven's gate to open wide;
He will wash away my sin; Let His little child come in.
Yes, Jesus loves me! Yes, Jesus loves me!
Yes, Jesus loves me! The Bible tells me so.

-Traditional Words: Anna B. Warner, Music: Wm. B. Bradbury

Ever-Green

I had a dream of evergreens
I planted in good soil.
I could see that every tree
was worthy of my toil.
I, drawing near, began to fear
my little trees were cursed.
Ten thousand weeds from hidden seeds
the enemy disbursed.

I could never pull each weed,
the evil one had sown.
I must wait, accept my fate,
'til trees were fully grown.
And then a voice from heaven
broke my anguish and my fear.
**"Let them grow, this evil foe
can't kill when I am near.**

**Watch closely until harvest,
I'll send servants unto you,
to do their deeds, pull the weeds;
Permit your trees to grow.
They will bind weeds into sheaves,
toss them in the waiting fire.
They will burn, I confirm,
these worthless weeds acquired.**

**Your trees must now be nourished;
these trees you have esteemed.
They will grow, this I know.
I'll keep them ever-green."**

"Let them both grow until the harvest. At that time I will tell the harvesters: First collect the weeds and tie them in bundles to be burned; then gather the wheat and bring it into the barn." Matthew 13:30 NIV

I Don't Know Your Mary

I have not met your all-consenting,
Mild, meek, passive handmaiden
Held captive, raped, impregnated
By a vicious, violent God.
I'm glad, so very glad.

I looked for her in Luke; she was not there.
Your mild Mary was in hiding; my Mary quite visible,
A young maiden "greatly troubled," not by the potential of abuse,
But for being hailed, "O favored one."

Nor from my vantage point could I see
Your Mary's passivity.
I saw involvement, frightened but not forced.
Fear of angel assault? Surely not.
Reassurance does not come from the enemy.

I'm quite sure she was not gagged or bound,
As questions from her lips
Were welcomed and allowed.
"How can this be?" (She asked legitimately)
"since I have no husband?"

Your Mary had no choice but to surrender to your god.
My Mary was chosen, surrender not required,
Only yieldedness.
Your Mary was a victim of a woman-hater god;
Mine a vehicle for the unfolding of a miracle.

Your Mary was violated by a holy rapist,
Mine blessed within her womb,
Each Messianic labor pain an offering
For the Redeemer of mankind.

From your emptiness, you ask,
"Was Mary ever self-possessed
A true virgin, a free spirit,

Dancing and touching and loving her sisters?"

From the fullness of her spirit,
My Mary gives a knowing nod,
Recalls her leap of faith consent, not rape, but rapture,
"...let it be to me according to your Word."

Her quiet answer follows without shame:
"My son died that we need not be self-possessed, but Spirit possessed,
Yes, to dance and touch, and love." *

(*written in response to another poem, printed in a college newspaper, with an opposite opinion about Mary, the mother of Jesus.)

"But the angel said to her, 'Do not be afraid, Mary; you have found favor with God. You will conceive and give birth to a son, and you are to call him Jesus. He will be great and will be called the Son of the Most High. The Lord will give him the throne of his father, David, and he will reign over Jacob's descendants forever; his kingdom will never end.'" Luke 1:30-33

Awesome Reach

God's arm is not shortened to save,
it reaches from birth to the grave.
Doesn't give up, on those who will trust
his creative talents with dust.

Angels he summons in line,
to assist him before and behind
the length of his bionic arm,
to hear and respond to alarm.

The Father, the Spirit, the Son,
lending compassion as One;
Fingers of grace, touching each face,
arms that encircle, embrace.

My arms can encircle one child,
And I know even one is worthwhile.
But thousands and more, sound the alarm;
and God stretches his Tri-onic Arm.

"Sing to the Lord a new song, for he has done marvelous things; his right hand and his holy arm have worked salvation for him. The Lord has made his salvation known and revealed his righteousness to all the nations." Psalms 98:1-2 NIV

Child of Mine

"Child of mine, lovest thou me?"
"Why, Yes, Lord, I love Thee!"
"With thy whole heart, lovest me true?"
I hesitate, then "Yes, of course, my whole heart too!"
"Then go to the pastures, feed my sheep,
with eyes wide open; you dare not sleep."

A second time I hear Him speak:
"Lovest thou me?" (From out of the deep.)
"Why do you ask? You know I do."
"With whole heart and soul, do you?"
"Yes… I think…I hope…I know
wherever you go, my spirit goes too!"
"Feed my lambs and hold them dear;
tell my flock to have no fear."

Thrice I hear him, "Lovest thou me?"
"Again You ask? Surely you see!"
"But with whole mind and strength do you,
in season and without still true?"
"Oh Lord, I try…but fail to love;
my strength and mind are not enough.
Yet I vow to feed your sheep
with spirit willing, flesh so weak.

"*…Jesus said to Simon Peter, 'Simon, Son of John, do you love me more than these others?' 'Yes,' Peter replied, 'You know that I am your friend.' 'Then feed my lambs,' Jesus told him. Jesus repeated the question: 'Simon, son of John, do you really love me?' 'Yes, Lord,' Peter said, 'You know that I am your friend.' 'Then take care of my sheep,' Jesus said. Once more he asked him, 'Simon, son of John, are you even my friend?' Peter was grieved at the way Jesus asked the question this third time. 'Lord, you know my heart; you know I am,' he said. Jesus said, 'Then feed my sheep.'" John 21:15-17 LB (paraphrased)*

Is Anything Too Hard for God?

Is anything too hard for God,
who formed a world in space,
who made the sun, the moon, the stars,
began the human race?

Is anything beyond His power
to rescue and to save,
he who rules the hearts of men,
majestic tidal wave?

Is anything removed so far
from Godly intervention,
his lengthy arm can't reach
to give it his attention?

Was not his love sufficient
to sacrifice for sin,
his one begotten Son?
Yes, this was hard for Him!

"The Lord answered Moses, 'Is the Lord's arm too short? Now you will see whether or not what I say will come true for you.'" Numbers 11:23 NIV

"For God so loved the world that he gave his one and only Son, that whoever believes in him shall not perish but have eternal life." John 3:16 NIV

Bethlehem of Judah

Oh Bethlehem of Judah, how could they call you least
among the ancient cities, the pathway to God's peace?
How could they miss the magnitude of David's royal city,
the manger for the King of Kings, salvation at God's bidding?

Stable friends bowed down to him, and shepherds from afar;
Wise men knelt in worship, for they had seen the star.
So quietly he came to earth, prophetic gift of heaven,
fulfillment of his holy Word, and by his Spirit driven.

Low in rank O Bethlehem? Of little consequence?
You still rock the cradle of sacred providence.
Our Christmas gifts and lights, joy and family feasts
celebrate the Savior's birth, the GREATEST gift - not least!

"But you Bethlehem, Ephrathah, though you are small among the clans of Judah, out of you will come for me one who will be ruler over Israel. Whose origins are from of old from ancient times." Micah 5:2 NIV

From My Grandchildren:
"My Christmas Wish" by Molly Tiede, 5th Grade…
For all of the soldiers to be home …then people won't have to worry about them getting hurt…that murderers will get caught and go to jail. People won't have to worry about gun fires.

No one will get killed….everyone would get at least one gift for Christmas. Even if they are poor, they will get one gift…Everyone will have a home. People don't have to stay out in the cold. They won't get sick and die. They also will be warm all of the time.

"My Christmas Wish" by Adrianna Tiede, 4th Grade
If I could have a wish, it would be for everybody to have at least one present and to see their family, because some people don't get to see their family for holidays. Some people don't even get any presents for any holidays like Christmas or Easter.

Trust and Obey

Simple words "trust" and "obey
Stirring words to heed each day.
Lean not on your intellect;
His greatest good you can expect.

Have confidence he will prevail;
Describe your needs in great detail.
Then leaning back, relaxing, wait.
His best answer's never late.

Dry your tears and comb your hair;
God is just, he'll treat you fair.
Sometimes it yet can seem unclear;
He knows best, so have no fear!

Trust is first and then obey!
Must not walk on feet of clay.
We must love his every word,
Seek his kingdom, self deferred.

He by his Spirit sends us forth
To spread his Word upon the earth.
Let Him hear your fervent plea:
"Here I am, Lord, please send me."

"Then I heard the voice of the Lord saying 'Whom shall I send? And whom will go for us?' And I said, 'Here am I. Send me!'" Isaiah 6:8 NIV

Whispering Thoughts

Give God your murmurs of allegiance,
your sighs of gratitude,
your quiet breaths of yieldedness.

Disclose with promised words
and whispers,
the fullness of your heart,
The simplicity of your faith;
your readiness
to hear him whisper in return.
Then wait.

"I wait for the Lord, my whole being waits, and in his word I put my hope. I wait for the Lord more than watchmen wait for morning; more that watchmen wait for morning." Psalms 130:5-6 NIV

"God whispers to us in our pleasures, speaks in our conscience, but shouts in our pain." C. S. Lewis

Mary's Child

"Soon," said Mary from her bed of hay,
through labored pain on this blessed day,
yielding herself to God's plan and will.
Bright were the stars; the evening was still.
Animals watched from rafters and floor.
The moon peeked down through the open door.

"Soon," said the mother, 'neath sweat and tears;
the little one comes, my time is here.
Then piercing cries from Madonna and child,
this moment not meek, this moment not mild.
Joseph leaned down to swaddle the babe.
He gazed at Mary, the Lord's handmaid.

"Now," said Mary as she drifted to sleep.
She trusted the angels, her child to keep.
She dreamed of the newborn, blest Savior on earth,
with shepherds and wise men attending his birth.
"Yes," said Mary, "He belongs to the world,"
as the little one slumbered, snuggled and curled.

God spoke to her heart of patience and love,
the price she would pay for this gift from above.
"Yes," on her lips as she woke from her dream,
cradled her infant with arms that would lean
on God the Almighty for strength to abide,
courage to carry the load God assigned.

"I am the Lord's servant," Mary answered. "May your word to me be fulfilled. Then the angel left her." Luke 1:38b NIV

"But Mary treasured up all these things and pondered them in her heart..." Luke 2:19 NIV

Come Walk with Me

Come, walk with me to Gethsemane;
come, do not be afraid.
I would have you to know this journey below,
the price that I willingly paid.

Come walk with me, I want you to see
how I stood accused before men.
Despising the shame, I died in your name,
the final atonement for sin.

They laughed and they jeered each time I appeared;
my heart showed compassion and love.
Then I went away to the garden to pray,
and plead with my Father above.

It was so dark, yet I knew from the start
my hour had finally come.
I was lost and alone, so far from God's throne,
yet I prayed, "Thy Will be done."

I carried your cross; in sin you were lost.
I was obedient to death.
I, in the end, was rejected by men.
"It is finished." I drew my last breath.

If you're following me to Gethsemane,
be prepared to drink of the cup.
You, too, will suffer, my sister and brother;
for me, you will give yourself up.

"Then Jesus said to his disciples, 'Whoever wants to be my disciple must deny themselves and take up their cross and follow me. For whoever wants to save their life will lose it, but whoever loses their life for me will find it."
Matthew 16:24-25 NIV

Remedy for Sin

Though cleaning agents activate
the soil deep within;
I question their effectiveness
upon the stains of sin.

Some products will, without a doubt,
give floors their proper sheen,
but I suspect a grudge won't budge
by using MR. CLEAN.

And wouldn't it be easy,
a most convenient route,
to stand before your bitterness,
and firmly SHOUT IT OUT?

Or when evil thoughts control you,
and you want to show who's boss,
wouldn't it be silly
to turn to SPRAY AND WASH?

These products, I won't argue,
are proven household friends;
but never were they advertized
a remedy for sin.

There is a stain remover,
can't be purchased anywhere.
Your garments will whitest
when you turn to God in prayer.

"Cleanse me with hyssop, and I will be clean; wash me, and I will be whiter than snow…Hide your face from my sins and blot out all my iniquity,"
Psalms 51:7, 9 NIV

Soooooo Big!

A mother may say to a child, "Soooooo Big,"
as she stretches her arms
as far as they will go.

Today I say of our God, "Sooooo Big!"
I can only ponder his big-ness.
this mighty and awesome God ,
who keeps his covenant of love
with his people.
Soooooo Big!

Performance has its limits
but bound-less is the arm of God.
He reaches higher than the highest mountain,
deeper than the deepest sea.
He gave, without murmur,
his son's life for me!
Soooooo Big!

"I will sing of the Lord's great love forever, with my mouth I will make your faithfulness known to all generations." Psalms 89:1 NIV

Sweet Peace

Sweet peace that I know in my heart here below,
sweet peace, that gift from above.
Though the world knows no peace,
and the wars never cease,
I'm blessed with this gift of His love.

For the world doesn't know the peace that can flow
when you're born of the Spirit of God.
And the world can't receive for their hearts won't believe;
the path that they travel is broad.

Sweet Spirit of peace, may your love never cease;
may it soften the hearts of all men.
May they turn from their way, and receive you today,
and be washed in the blood of the Lamb.

Then they will know the peace that can flow
from the Christ who died for their sin.
This peace they can claim, since he died in their name,
a lifetime of peace to bestow.

"...and he will be called Wonderful Counselor, Mighty God, Prince of Peace. Everlasting Father." Isaiah 9:6b NIV

"A heart at peace gives life to the body." Proverbs 14:30a NIV

Resting in Jehovah

Do you desire healing? Is your body weak, infirm?
Seek Jehovah-rophe, your healing to affirm.

If you want to stretch a banner for all to see God's love,
spell out Jehovah-nissi and fly it like a dove.

When you need God's tender mercies; and your heart is broken, raw,
lay them at the shepherd's feet; rest in Jehovah-raah.

When you need provisions, God will calm your fear.
Simply lift your voices to Jehovah-jireh.

Are challenges too great?
Do you sag and moan?
Are you chasing after peace?
Shout out Jehovah-shalom!

"Guide me oh thou great Jehovah, pilgrim through this barren land.
I am weak, but you are mighty, hold me with your powerful hand.
Bread of heaven, bread of heaven, feed me now and evermore.
Feed me now and evermore.

Open now the crystal fountain, where the healing waters flow;
Let the fire and cloudy pillar lead me all my journey through.
Strong deliverer, strong deliverer, shield me with your mighty arm.
Shield me with your mighty arm."

-Hymn, Guide Me Oh Thou Great Jehovah" Text: William Williams, Tune: John Hughes

Wandering

Wandering in the wilderness,
forty years or more,
letting Moses lead them
to that far and distant shore.
They were led.
They were fed.
They received their daily bread.

Wandering in the wilderness
so very far from home,
drained them of their victory;
they grumbled and they moaned.
They were led.
They were fed.
They received their daily bread.

Wandering in the wilderness
they turned away from Him,
worshipping a golden calf
and leading lives of sin.
They disobeyed; still were slaves,
for their sins they paid.

They wandered in the wilderness
and did not pass God's test.
and thus, they were forbidden
to enter in His rest.
They sighed; they cried.
They died,
unsatisfied.

"...not one of those who saw my glory and the signs I performed in Egypt and in the wilderness but who disobeyed me and tested me ten times—not one of them will ever see the land I promise on an oath to their ancestors..." Numbers 14:22 NIV

Peace Beyond Understanding

May the peace that passes human understanding
guard and keep your minds on Jesus Christ our Lord.
Oh, the peace that passes human understanding
is our reward for sins our Savior bore.

This peace has calmed the hearts that once were troubled;
this peace has stilled the waters that were rough.
Once you've received this lasting peace from Jesus,
this peace – this staying peace, will be enough.

No description of this peace can be given.
No definition I have heard has been complete.
If you want the peace that passes understanding;
repent and leave your sins at Jesus' feet.

You will know the grace of your blessed Redeemer
and his love and joy forever will abound.
You will have met the precious Lord and Savior,
and the simple peace you sought, you will have found.

"Peace I leave with you; my peace I give you. I do not give to you as the world gives. Do not let your hearts be troubled and do not be afraid." John 14:27 NIV

Our God is Not a Wasteful God

Our God is not a wasteful God;
he uses everything....
grief-stricken hearts, tears that burn,
stubborn hurts that cling.

Burdensome relationships,
betrayals of our trust,
Handicaps of mind and limb;
shattered dreams in dust.

Abuse of body, soul and mind,
loneliness and fear,
persecution for his sake;
and needless sin we bear.

Surrender all to him who seeks
justice everywhere,
blesses souls who trust in him;
and does their burdens bear.

It may not happen in a day,
or even in a year,
But he will work his will to do;
little ones draw near.

Our God is not a wasteful God;
let your suffering spirit sing.
He will exchange your ills for good,
so bring him everything!

"Those who trust in the Lord are like Mt. Zion, which cannot be shaken, but endures forever. As the mountains surround Jerusalem, so the Lord surrounds his people both now and forevermore." Psalms 125:1-2 NIV

Fear Not Little Flock

Fear not, little flock, fear not.
It is indeed God's pleasure
to give you the kingdom;
He offers you this gift of love.
Fear not!

The kingdom is like a hidden treasure
a man sold everything to buy.
The field was full of riches,
and he, one happy guy.
Fear not!

One day an avid seeker
found a pearl of great price,
quickly sold all he owned;
this pearl saved his life.
Fear not!

The kingdom, like a heavy net,
lifts fish from out the sea.
Many kept, from waters' depth,
will reach eternity.
Fear not!

Fear not little flock, fear not.
You're treasures in his sight,
You're the sheep of his pasture,
In whom his soul delights.
Fear not!

"and there shall be one flock and one shepherd." John 10:16b NIV

"He tends his flock like a shepherd; he gathers the lambs in his arms and carries them close to his heart; he gently leads those who have young." Isaiah 40:11 NIV

The Log

Do not see slivers of evil,
nor think of your brother as cursed.
Look hard at yourself before judging;
lift the log from your own eye first.

Do not hate the one who has wronged you,
though his life shows what he has sown.
Just think about how to remove IT,
that rotten log in your own.

If it's too large to be budged,
too stubborn to even be loosed,
may God send his angels with tools
to drill out that sinful log first.

Forget his slivers and specs;
fall down on your face before God.
Forgive your sisters and brothers,
surrender yourself – AND the log.

"Why do you look at the spec of sawdust in your brother's eye, with never a thought for the great plank in your own? Or how can you say to your brother, 'Let me take the spec out of your eye,' when all the time there is a plank in your own? You hypocrite! First take the plank out of your own eye, and then you will see clearly to take the spec out of your brother's." Matthew 7:3-5 NEB

He Careth for You

Cast all your cares upon Him;
he careth deeply for you.
Bring him your grief and your sorrow;
he labors to make all things new.

You are weak and so weary;
trust him to strengthen each day.
You can abide in his glory;
I know he will show you the way.

He can turn ashes to beauty;
he can turn tears into hope.
He will assure you so sweetly;
his Word will help you to cope.

He'll gather your tears into bottles;
your suffering, he'll nail to the cross.
He died for your sin and your sorrow;
he's weeping, bemoaning your loss.

"To comfort all who mourn, and provide for those who grieve in Zion, to bestow on them a crown of beauty instead of ashes, the oil of joy instead of mourning, and a garment of praise instead of a spirit of despair. Isaiah 61:3a NIV

"Thou hast keep count of my tossings; put thou my tears in thy bottle! Are they not in thy book?" Psalms 56:4 RSV

Are You Walking with Jesus?

Are you walking with Jesus one day at a time,
or are you so busy that he's left behind?
When troubles surround you and darkness sets in,
when you feel all alone, are you trusting in him?

When anger takes over, disturbs peace of mind,
perhaps in that moment you've left Christ behind.
When jealousy tempts you and envy torments;
are your eyes on Jesus and his righteousness?

When harsh words are spoken, white lies that deceive;
do you cry out in sorrow to the Spirit you've grieved?
When you close your eyes to injustice and wrong;
can you honestly say that to God you belong?

When you fail to show others his wondrous love,
can you be a child of the Father above?
Are you walking with Jesus one day at a time,
or are there some moments you've left him behind?

"…looking unto Jesus, the author and finisher of our faith…"
Hebrews 12:2 NKJV

"but those who hope in the Lord will renew their strength. They will soar on wings like eagles; they will run and not grow weary, they will walk and not be faint."
Isaiah 40:31 NIV

Damascene Pigeons (New Beginnings)

The Damascene Pigeons originated somewhere in the Middle East, though exactly where is lost in the mists of time. Even in the 17th century it was regarded as an old breed. Its two most striking features are the dark plum eye ceres and its bright eyes. Although it is an exhibition breed in modern times, they were developed for flight and still do best if they get a fair amount of flying exercise. The Damascene is still a rare breed in the US.

Barry Koffler, Feathersite.com

The Apostle Paul, or Saul, as he called, when he was persecuting the Christians, had some excitement on the road to Damascus. He was blinded by a bright light from heaven and heard the voice of Jesus say, "Saul, Saul, why do you persecute me?" When God healed his eye sight, scales fell from his eyes. It could not have been a pretty sight. He was not attractive like the Damascene, but he became more attractive on the inside as God changed his heart. Later he began to preach the gospel of Christ. During his missionary journeys, he got in a lot of "flying time" for the Lord! Damascus became the scene of his new beginning, as he was converted to Christianity.

New Beginning

Today's a new beginning;
God is watching over me.
He will keep my tongue from slander
as his Spirit flows through me.

Harsh words will not be spoken;
he will give me self-control.
His gentle, quiet Spirit
today will be my goal.

God's looking o'er my shoulder;
he will keep me from all sin.
He'll steer me from temptation
if I keep my eyes on him.

I'm trusting God for patience
for this day fresh and new;
God has given me the will
and he will work to do.

"Like a city whose walls are broken is a person who lacks self-control."
Proverbs 25:28 NIV

"make every effort to add to your faith goodness, knowledge, self-control, perseverance, Godliness, mutual affection, love." 2 Peter 1:5-7 NIV

Pruning

Christ has explained in great detail
(His Holy Spirit will vouch.)
My response repeats the strain,
"Ouch, and ouch, and ouch!

I am ever willing, Lord,
to start from scratch again,
if you will fertilize my faith;
remind me where I've been.

I will remain as you remain;
I will abide in you.
I cannot do all this alone,
So, stick to me like glue.

I do not want to wither, Lord,
or be consumed by fire.
I do not wish my fruit to rot;
I want your heart's desire.

I want to bring you glory, Lord,
grow fruit that makes you proud.
Prune me, if you have to, Lord;
forgive me when I scream out loud!

"He cuts off every branch in me that bears no fruit, while every branch that does bear fruit he prunes so that it will be even more fruitful…Remain in me as I also remain in you. No branch can bear fruit by itself; it must remain in the vine. Neither can you bear fruit unless you remain in me." John 15:2, 4 NIV

Occupation

Hate occupied the heart of Saul, hate inspired his mission;
Hatred and self-righteousness were plots to kill the Christians.
He sought them with a vengeance and many followed him;
He obeyed the Jewish laws, was a Roman citizen.

He sanctioned stoning Stephen, a Godly man of grace.
He justified the violence and soon forgot his face.
Satan had a greater deed for Saul to undertake;
Conspiring with officials to consummate his hate.

Warrants of arrest for Christians in Damascus,
Hate was in those papers; death was in the dust.
Saul, obsessed, perhaps possessed, by demons in disguise,
Would come to know the holy glow of God who occupies.

Modern Sauls, in schools halls, strike out to kill and maim.
The settings may be different; the evil still the same.
Satan steals and occupies the hearts of fallen men.
He whispers to his henchmen to stand and follow him.

They're ripe for all his rotten lies and follow right behind.
It happened not too long ago in a place called Columbine.
Guns left victims in the wake and grief that stunned the town.
Blood was on minds of boys to strike the Christians down.

Many talk of gun control to turn the tide of crime,
Background checks and the effects of guns to undermine.
But what of hearts and hatred that tear our world apart,
At war with hearts of Christian love and kindness to impart?

Saul was changed, turned inside-out;
He heard the Savior's cry,
Put off the old, put on the new,
Chose God to occupy!

"For everyone born of God overcomes the world. This is the victory that has overcome the world, even our faith. Who is it that overcomes the world? Only the one who believes that Jesus is the Son of God." 1 John 4-5 NIV

"They triumphed over him by the blood of the lamb and by the word of their testimony." Revelation 12:11 NIV

Determined Stride

I know where I am going; I know from whence I came.
I know the God who changed my life; I'll never be the same.
Years have slowed my footsteps and I've stumbled on my pride;
He is the wind that whistles through my determined stride.

Oh wing me to the weary, the burdened and oppressed.
Give me words of wisdom and works of righteousness.
And when I start to weaken, am tested, torn and tried;
Still be the wind that whistles through my determined stride.

He gives me grace to follow; he stirs my feeble frame.
He is the God who changed my life; I'll never be the same.
The pace is not important, or when I, by faith, arrive,
But I must hear him whistle through my determined stride.

"I have been crucified with Christ, and I no longer live, but Christ lives in me. The life I now live in the body, I live by faith in the Son of God, who loved me and gave himself for me." Galatians 2:20 NIV

"For it is by grace you have been saved, through faith—and this is not from yourselves, it is the gift of God—not by works, so that no one can boast." Ephesians 2:8-9 NIV

The Second Mile

I stand before the second mile,
breathing deep and fast.
Sweat runs down my forehead;
don't think my strength will last.

I know what lies ahead of me;
I know what I must do.
Still, I rest from that first mile,
too weak to follow you.

"Sufficient is my grace," I hear,
while trying hard to stand.
With face turned toward Jerusalem,
I see your outstretched hand.

Reluctantly, at first, I go,
to heal some hurting hearts.
offer my apologies
with grace that you impart.

I face a wall, then hear you call:
"You must help the poor and needy.
their burdens weigh them down
and Christians can't be greedy.

The lonely wait just down the road,
broken, grieving, sad.
Step up your pace, and in God's grace,
You'll make their spirits glad.

The second mile takes sacrifice;
the second mile takes faith.
You will never travel alone;
I'll match you pace by pace."

Because I know You always go
the second mile with me.

So with your Spirit leading,
perhaps I can make three.

"But one thing I do: Forgetting what is behind and straining toward what is ahead, I press on toward the goal to win the prize for which God has called me heavenward in Christ Jesus. Philippians 3:12b NIV

"The race is not to the swift or the battle to the strong, nor does food come to the wise or wealth to the brilliant, or favor to the learned." Ecclesiastes 9:12 NIV

The Master Mender

Please stop and take another look
before you throw that cup away.
Examine closely every flaw,
do not fling your life away.

Are you sure it's not worth saving?
Without a doubt beyond repair?
Could it possibly be mended
with patience and with care?

I know the Master Mender;
He's passing by today.
Ask for his appraisal;
hear what he has to say.

His advice is well worth having;
He's experienced in the art
of mending broken lives
and restoring empty hearts.

You will listen to the Master
and believe his words are true,
If the broken life you're holding
means anything to you.

He has mended many broken cups
with cracks so deep and wide,
you would marvel at the mastery
if you would look inside.

The ugliest of the ugly,
he has given beauty rare.
The rejects of this world
he's restored beyond compare.

There still is time to gather up
the pieces that you hold,
and view before your very eyes
this cup - your life, made whole.

From my Journal :

"...*As I was working on my quilt last night it took on a spiritual character, even in its construction. I was thinking of brokenness, of how a broken person can truly experience the grace of God. Only in brokenness can we cry out to God—only in our storms at sea (name of quilt pattern) are we willing to cry out to God, 'Save me else I perish?' We are tested beyond endurance, stretched to the limits of our own power. As I was sewing the pieces, I saw myself in the hands of a righteous and loving God...as he bought the broken pieces of my life together in a pleasing pattern—like my quilt.*"

From Glory unto Glory

He changes, rearranges me
from glory unto glory.
He patiently provides
with a new and blessed story.

I am a new creation built on his foundation;
my life that was is now forever gone.
The new is full of glory;
I am singing his new song.

I am moving higher by Spirit and by fire;
my steps are slow, unsteady in his eyes.
From glory unto glory
I will rise.

His Spirit is so patient; His love is ever gracious.
He holds my hand and gently raises me;
from glory unto glory
I am free.

His Kingdom is forever.
He will leave me never;
I'll walk each step of glory undefiled.
And when He calls my name I will smile.

And my God will meet all your needs according to the riches of his glory In Christ Jesus." Philippians 4:19 NIV

Whiter Than Snow

I stripped off my garments of sin,
stood naked and bare before Him.
Ashamed and guilty I came
What possible good could I claim?

I buried my head and I cried.
I knew that for me he had died.
I looked at the soil and the stain;
So sorry I could not abstain.

He took my garments, obscene;
touched them and they were made clean.
Relieved of my burden of sin,
I fell down on my knees before him.

"Worthy is the Lamb, who was slain, to receive power, and wealth and wisdom and strength and honor and glory and praise." Revelation 5:13b NIV

He Leadeth Me

The Lord is my Shepherd; he calls me by name.
He knows like none other my sin and my shame.
I shall not want, not ever he says,
provider of substance beyond daily bread.

He makes me recline in pastures so green.
He gives needed rest; he watches unseen.
Beside quiet waters He bids me to come,
clearing the pathway, with obstacles none.

In need of refreshing, he restores my soul.
I'm a new person; I rock and I roll!
Along the right paths he keeps me secure;
prevents me from straying, gives grace to endure.

For his namesake he does this and more,
righteous and holy right down to the core.
Though walking the valley of darkness so grim,
he is before me; I'm following him.

I do not fear evil when I hold his hand.
He offers protection; he helps me to stand.
His rod and his staff, all the comfort I need,
his love's everlasting; I trust him to lead.

He sets up his table; my enemies flee.
He protects me, defends me, delivers me free.
Oil of gladness flows over my head.
Anointed for service, my fears have all fled.

Goodness and mercy will follow forever.
The rest of my life he leaves me never.
I will live – I will dwell, in the house of the Lord,
abiding with him, his favor outpoured.

He leadeth me;
He bends my knee.
I know my Shepherd
leadeth me.

"The Lord is the strength of his people, a fortress of salvation for his anointed one. Save your people and bless their inheritance; be their shepherd and carry them forever." Psalms 28:8-9 NIV

Higher Math

God has made the difference in my life,
adding and subtracting as he wills;
multiplying joy and countless blessing,
dividing pain and many digit ills.

My God has never dealt in theorems
or weak and lame hypotheses.
He is my formula for living;
his Word is truth as he decrees.

He's discovered errors in my figures;
corrected and supplied where I've erased.
God had tutored me in higher mathematics,
passed me only by his mercy and His grace.

"Take my yoke upon you and learn from me, for I am gentle and humble in heart, and you will find rest for your souls. For my yoke is easy and my burden is light." Matthew 11:29-30 NIV

"...let the wise listen and add to their learning; and let the discerning get guidance— for understanding proverbs and parables, the sayings and riddles of the wise." Proverbs 1:5-6 NIV

The House of the Lord

I rejoiced when they said unto me;
let us go to the house of the Lord.
We were out before the gates
where our spirits contemplate,
the beauty of the temple he restored.

I was glad when we entered his temple;
I recalled all his blessings to me.
His saving love is kind;
when he found me I was blind;
he opened up my eyes so I could see.

I was delighted to join with God's people,
ecstatic, exultant, consumed
by God ever present,
his love effervescent,
called Jesus to rise from the tomb.

I gave him my life at the altar,
Surrendered it fully to him.
He cast out my sin,
new life to begin;
I'm praising my God with a grin!

"I rejoiced with those who said to me, 'Let us go to the house of the Lord.' Our feet are standing in your gates, Jerusalem." Psalms 122:1-2 NIV

I Am the One

I am the One
Who leads you to green pastures to rest.
I am the One
Who removes weight from your heart and your soul.
Yes, I am the One.

I am the One
Who breathes new life into you.
I am the One
Who makes you, again, like new.
Yes, I am the One.

I am the One
Who speaks softly his Word.
I am the One
Who carries when you cannot walk.
Yes, I am the One.

I am the One
Who bids you to eat and to drink.
I am the One
Who anoints you with oil.
Yes, I am the One.

I am the One
Who meets you by quiet waters.
I am the One
Who causes your cup to overflow.
Yes, I am the One,
And I am here!

"The Lord is my shepherd, I shall not be in want." Psalm 23:1 NIV

"I am the Lord, and there is no other; apart from me there is no God. I will strengthen you." Isaiah 45:5a NIV

Holy of Holies

I entered the Holy of Holies,
was washed in the blood of the Lamb.
All of my sins were forgiven,
His child and forever I am.

I carried no gift to the altar.
He offered himself just for me,
the light of his presence so blinding,
the gift of his Spirit so free.

Spiritual sight was ignited;
He baptized me without fear.
I entered the Holy of Holies;
Jesus, my Savior was there.

"Therefore, brothers and sisters, since we have confidence to enter the Most Holy Place by the blood of Jesus, by a new and living way opened for us through the curtain, that is, his body, and since we have a great priest over the house of God, let us draw near to God with a sincere heart, and with the full assurance that faith brings, having our hearts sprinkled to cleanse us from a guilty conscience and having our bodies washed with pure water. Let us hold unswervingly to the hope we profess, for he who promised is faithful." Hebrews 10:19-23 NIV

God is Living

He is active, living and vital,
likewise, his work in our lives;
not a ruler who's absent,
but one who touches, revives.

His motion, energy, Spirit,
persistence, vitality, change,
goes deep in the hearts that are willing;
who answer God's call to engage.

The yoke of the Savior is easy;
his burden, he tells us, is light.
Link your load with the Savior;
walk with him into the light.

"In all my prayers for all of you, I always pray with joy because of your partnership in the gospel from the first day until now, being confident of this, that he who began a good work in you will carry it on to completion until the day of Christ Jesus." Philippians 1:4-6

Hungry Pigeons (and thirsty, too!)

Hungry Pigeons is not a species, but food is an inescapable necessity, likewise for us. Pigeons eat a lot of different things. They like a variety of grains and cereals, such as cracked corn, millet, wheat, etc. Seeds are a primary source of food. In the city they will scavenge on all sorts of leftovers and trash, much of which is not healthy for them. Pigeons like to eat whatever they can find, but tend to be vegetarian.

Christians are not spiritual vegetarians; they are after the meat, not the milk. They hunger for the deeper, richer things of God. They feed on his word. Jesus said that man cannot live on bread alone, but by every word that comes from the mouth of God. Sometimes we live on mustard seeds. By the grace of God they can grow, expand and flourish like the Kingdom of God. Other seeds that we digest are spiritual seeds from other believers. Jesus said, "Blessed are those who hunger and thirst for righteousness, for they will be filled." —Filled with joy in his presence. He also warns us to stay away from "junk food." In other words, don't stuff yourselves on that which is contrary to his will and plan for your lives. Don't forget to share your "good seeds" with others—they're hungry too! Eat the meat and throw the bones away.

Fishing with Jesus

I'd like to go fishing with Jesus
out on the Galilee Sea;
from morning 'til night, in darkness and light,
fishing, just Jesus and me.

I'd like to go fishing with Jesus
out in his old rugged boat;
in shallow, in deep, I know he will keep
me and my gear all afloat.

I'd like to go fishing with Jesus
sharing his lunch while at sea.
If a storm should arise, to him, no surprise;
so softly, he'll ask it to leave.

I'd like to go fishing with Jesus
for chatter, for challenge and more;
dropping our nets, then admiring our catch,
hauling it all back to shore.

I'd like to go fishing with Jesus,
I know that with him I'm complete.
Yes, I'm first in line to share in his wine,
When Jesus says "Come, let us eat!"

"Jesus said to them, 'Come and have breakfast.' None of the disciples dared ask him, 'Who are you?' They knew it was the Lord. Jesus came, took the bread, and gave it to them, and did the same with the fish. This was now the third time Jesus appeared to his disciples since he was raised from the dead." John 21:12-14 NIV

Very Pregnant

We are very pregnant
With the Words of God.
He planted seed within us
He only gave his nod.
Pregnant with His wisdom;
His new life entered in.
He fertilized and germanized
To make us more like him.

He knew our baby appetites,
Rich milk from His breast.
He raised us up to solid food;
He helped us to digest.
We are getting fatter
As we eat and drink His Word,
Food that does not perish,
To heaven it endures.

We know He is our Father.
Do we look like Him?
Is there enough resemblance?
Do we have his chin?

"Do not work for the food that spoils, but for the food that endures to eternal life, which the Son of Man will give you. For on him God the Father has placed his seal of approval." John 6:27 NIV

A Glutton for Living Water

Never drink of my Spirit
Like a regent sipping her tea,
Holding her cup by two fingers,
Tasting it, so daintily.

Thrust your head in my Fountain;
Drink like a glutton for more.
Ten gallons of my Holy Spirit,
Mighty, tremendous, outpour.

Sipping is counterproductive,
It surely will dry on your lips.
I'm offering free living water;
Gushing and rushing, no sips.

"Let anyone who is thirsty come to me and drink. Whoever believes in me, as Scripture has said, rivers of living water will flow out from within them."
John 7:37b NIV

Needy

How little I need of worldly things;
great is my need
for remission of sins.

How little it takes to feed me each day;
great is my hunger
for truth and His way.

My body needs little to clothe and to dress;
I'll always be greedy
for righteousness.

Unnecessary is the praise of men;
great is my need
to be exalted by Him.

"But seek first his kingdom and his righteousness, and all these things will be given to you as well." *Matthew 6:33 NIV*

New Year

New Years' Day passes quietly
as easy as turning a page
pausing to recall events
of the last chapter
looking forward
to the next
with excitement
and curiosity.

Hungry for dancing words
inspiring phrases
strong verbs
sentences of life
that question
exclaim, exhort
leaving no doubt or fear
where the periods should be.

"But as it is written, what no eye has seen, nor ear heard, nor the heart of man conceived, what God has prepared for those who love him." 1 Corinthians 2:9 RSV

"and he who sat upon the throne makes all things new. Also he said, 'write this, for these words are trustworthy and true.'" Revelation 21:5 NIV

You Speak to Me in Poetry

You speak to me in poetry,
a language we both know.
You in heavenly dialect,
and I of earth below.

You never scold my ignorance,
You just open up your Book,
and we go through our ABC's,
'an maybe take another look.

When my mortal mind can't carry
all Your thoughts, and words and plans,
You say "Meet me here for dinner,
don't forget to wash your hands!"

"What we have received is not the spirit of the world, but the Spirit who is from God, so that we may understand what God has freely given us." 1 Corinthians 2:12 NIV

Questions

Lord, you know I'm full of questions
about your holy Word.
The world is full of answers,
that do not go unheard.

Answers parade before me,
all having bits of truth.
Still seeking more, I agonize;
it's like an aching tooth!

You can ease that aching tooth;
the process is most frugal.
Child of questioning agony,
have you not heard of Google?

"Be patient toward all that is unresolved in your heart. Try to love the questions themselves. Do not now seek the answers, which cannot be given because you would not be able to live them. And the point is to live everything. Live the questions now. Perhaps you will then gradually, without noticing it, live along some distant day into the answers." --Rainer Maria Rilke

"Blessed are those who find wisdom, those who gain understanding, for she is more profitable than silver and yields better returns than gold." Proverbs 3:13-14 NIV

Thy Word

Thy Word is like manna from heaven,
sent down to the starving` on earth.
Each day we are fed by this heavenly bread,
and satisfied souls prove its worth.

Thy Word is like manna from heaven,
fresh miracle manna each day.
Soon we discover thy Word will uncover;
replenish this food as we pray.

As the children of Israel hungered,
and were fed by the hand of the Lord;
we too can depend on our starving to end,
as we feast upon God's Holy Word.

Excerpt from <u>My Pigeon Heart</u> by Denise Slette

"Sit still little one." Mary laughed. "I'm still not done! Here's a small pouch of food to take with you on your journey home." "What kind of food?" I asked. "This is a very special kind of food that God Himself made for His people of Israel, when they were wandering in the desert. It's called 'manna.'"… "The pouch of manna will never go empty! You and your friends will have your fill. You'll never be hungry again! Your heavenly Father will provide for you. He will keep your manna pouch full."

The Wine of Your Word

I should have listened to Jesus,
when he said old wine skins won't do.
I sewed with patience and skill,
patches wide and worn through.

I should have listened to Jesus,
not wasted the wine of good news;
should have tossed that old wineskin
before bursting the seams I had sewed,

Offer me, Lord, your new wineskin;
fill it with wine of your Word.
Give me to drink of your wisdom;
Let my spirit be stirred.

I'll try to be true to your calling,
waste not a drop of new wine,
allow it to nurture my spirit;
leaving old wineskins behind.

"Neither do people pour new wine into old wineskins, If they do, the skins will burst; the wine will run out and the wineskins will be ruined. No, they pour new wine into new wineskins, and both are preserved." Matthew 9:17 NIV

More of Jesus

More of Jesus! I want more!
Make his indwelling Spirit soar.
Lift me up on wings of fire,
Burning with my heart's desire.

More of Jesus! I want more!
His gentle Spirit at my core,
Loving as he first loved me,
Dressed in his humility.

More of Jesus! I want more!
Heart enthroned - His Word outpoured.
Holy Spirit, grant to me
More of Jesus,
less of me.

"He must become greater; I must become less." John 3:30 NIV

"I have come that they may have life, and have it to the full."
John 10:10b NIV

Living Words

Lord, why would I flee from thee?
You have the words of eternal life;
Living words that help me see
    The picture of eternity.

Words that comfort and sustain,
I store them deep within my heart;
Enduring words that shall remain,
    Never fail me nor depart.

Words of wisdom from the wise;
    Words of pardon for my sin.
    Words that open up my eyes,
Sharing love and discipline.

Words that fill my hungry soul,
Quench my thirst for righteousness.
Words that mend and make me whole,
    Words of caution and caress.

Ancient words of prophecy,
Keep me watchful and aware.
Words of power and energy,
    To restore and to repair.

Never, ever would I flee
From burning words of life within,
Words that have me running free.
Words eternal, words that win.

"My son, if you accept my words and store up my command within you, turning your ear to wisdom and applying your heart to understanding—indeed, if you call out for insight and cry aloud for understanding, and if you look for it as for silver and search for it as for hidden treasure, then you will understand the fear of the Lord and find the knowledge of God. Proverbs 2:1-5

My Joy is Leaking, Lord

My spirit's slow to start these days,
when once my engine roared.
I'm not sure I'll make the hill;
my joy is leaking, Lord.

I putt-putt-putt, when I should purr,
repairs I can't afford.
I don't maintain my usual speed;
my joy is leaking, Lord.

I checked the tires, filled the tank
(but the engine I ignored).
Do you know where I can find
a good mechanic, Lord?

"Not that I have already obtained all this, or have already arrived at my goal, but I press on to take hold of that for which Christ Jesus took hold of me...but one thing I do: forgetting what is behind and straining toward what is ahead, I press on toward the goal to win the prize for which God has called me heavenward in Christ Jesus." Philippians 3:12-14 NIV

Tree of Life

I long to be that stately tree
whose leaves shall never wither.
I long to be that fruitful tree
that grows beside the river.

To never lack for nourishment,
to never lack for health,
To grow and prosper every day
in Godly, righteous wealth.

To let my roots go down so deep
within your fertile ground;
to know the source I feed upon
forever will abound.

Lord, let me be that well-fed tree
whose leaves shall never wither;
let me bear much fruit for you
along that winding river.

"That person is like a tree planted by streams of water, which yields its fruit in season and whose leaf does not wither – whatever they do prospers." Psalms 1:3 NIV

"So then, just as you received Christ Jesus as Lord, continue to live your lives in him, rooted and built up in him, strengthened in the faith…" Colossians 2:6-7 NIV

The Hem of His Garment

I trailed the crowd that followed Him,
unable to keep pace.
His back was always turned to me;
I could not see his face.

Others pushed, hurried by,
calling out to him.
Begging him for healing,
left me behind again.

If only I could touch his hem,
dragging in the dust;
reach the tassels with my hand,
not causing any fuss.

I would surely feel his power,
surging like his love.
If I could only catch his hem;
He'd end this flow of blood.

Once more, I struggled forward,
reaching out again.
With joy I felt his dusty robe;
my fingers brushed the hem!

"But Jesus said, 'someone touched me; I know that power has gone out from me.' Then the woman seeing that she could not go unnoticed, came trembling and fell at his feet. In the presence of all people, she told them why she had touched him and how she had been healed. Then he said to her, 'Daughter, your faith has healed you; go in peace.'" Luke 8:46-48 NIV

I Want to See Your Face

I've seen Your hands reaching toward me;
I've felt your feet on my path.
I've experienced your goodness and mercy;
the quantified love that thou hath.

I've tasted your bread from heaven;
I've sensed you praying with me.
I'm blessed by your Holy Spirit;
I'm living and walking with thee.

Though all of these blessings I treasure,
and none would I want to erase;
but, oh God, my Father in heaven,
when will I see your dear face?

"My heart says of you, 'Seek his face!' Your face, Lord, I will seek." Psalms 27:8 NIV

"There he was transfigured before them. His face shone like the sun, and his clothes became as white as the light," Matthew 17:2 NIV

Emmaus Road

Did not His words within us burn?
they voiced to one another.
He opened up the Scriptures;
He taught us like none other.

We did not recognize his face,
this newly risen Christ.
His voice was not familiar;
yet his words enticed.

Later, breaking bread with him,
his words were ringing true.
His Spirit hovered over us;
in retrospect, we knew.

Christ was like a torch in them,
breathing holy fire.
His words were lit by angels,
sparking bold desire.

I'm longing for that fire, Lord,
the burning of your Word;
Hold my hand and walk with me
down my Emmaus road.

"'Is not my word like fire,' declares the Lord...." *Jeremiah 23:29a NIV*

"But I say, 'I will not mention his word or speak anymore in his name,' his word is in my heart like a fire, a fire shut up in my bones. I am weary of holding it in; Indeed, I cannot." *Jeremiah 20:9 NIV*

Leavened Bread

I was just a lump of dough formed by the Master's touch.
Until he held me in his hand, I really wasn't much.
He smothered me with flour, and patted tenderly.
He seized me and he squeezed me, shaped me lovingly.

Far beyond my boundaries he stretched with giant hands.
He folded me within his grace; he smiled knowingly.
I could not see what I would be, was still a lump of dough.
He covered me with grace so he could watch me grow.

I felt a stirring deep within like it was heaven-sent;
I could know 'twas holy dough with God's ingredients.
I found myself expanding with ever widening haste;
surmising I was rising by the Spirit's quickening pace.

By leaven of God's Spirit I was changing from a lump;
raising up and praising up, growing rather plump.
I was ready to surrender to the heat of discipline.
Keep me rising, keep me thriving; let the bread begin!

I wasn't much to start with Lord, just a tiny hump.
You leavened me, and heavened me; you slowly raised me up.
You've baked me with your blessing, my rough edges you endured.
Now help me feed the hungry, those starving for your Word.

"But you shouldn't be so concerned about perishable things like food. No, spend your energy seeking the eternal life that I can give you…" John 6:27 LB (paraphrased)

Rock Pigeons

Wild rock doves, or pigeons, are pale grey with two black bars on each wing. Habitats include various open and semi-open environments. Cliff and rock ledges are used for roosting and breeding in the wild. They have a dark bluish-grey head, neck, chest with glossy, yellowish, greenish, and reddish purple iridescence along its neck and wing feathers. The iris is red, orange, or gold with a paler inner ring, and the bare skin around the eye is bluish grey. The feet are purplish-red. Although they are relatively strong fliers, they also glide frequently, holding their wings in a very pronounced V shape as they fly. It is a very common breed of pigeons. They are often seen in rocky cliffs, farmland and fields. **Rock dove, Wikipedia, The Free Encyclopedia,https:/en.wikiapedia.org/wiki/Rock_dove# Description**

Christians are God's common pigeons. He is our Rock, where we roost, are fed, grow, and learn to fly under his tutelage by the power of the Holy Spirit. As we grow in the Spirit, he allows his iridescent colors to rub off on us. Grace! In the Bible, God is often referred to as a "Rock," because he is solid, unchanging, and immovable. And in the words of the hymnist, we sing with gusto: "Built on a Rock the Church does stand, even when steeples are falling." Christ is our Rock!

He is My Rock

He is the Rock
On which I stand
Safe and secure
From sinking sand.

If I should slip
In raging tide
He reaches me
He lifts me high.

He carries me
To solid shore
He is my Rock
Forevermore.

I walk beyond
The foaming brine
Discover foot prints
In sands of time.

He is my Rock
Throughout each storm
He's sheltered me
Since I was born.

He is my Rock
On Him I stand
So I might see
The Fatherland.

"*He set my feet on a rock and gave me a firm place to stand.*" Psalms 40:2 NIV

Solid Foundation

Stunning bricks without mortar
will tumble swiftly down,
ruining the foundation,
littering the ground.
Life without God
will crumble in decay,
rob you of his staying power,
as it slowly sinks away.

You'll need some mighty masonry,
water, lime and sand,
stirred with all the powers of heaven,
mortar to withstand
Prevailing winds, the 'tempters' snare,
the warring factors wild;
all of life's uncertainties,
set up to be defiled.

Mix the water of God's Spirit,
the sand of discipline,
blending in the lime of love
and do not spread too thin.
Your foundation will be solid;
it will stand forever firm.
It will be sealed forever,
faultless to overturn.

"They are like a man building a house, who dug down deep and laid the foundation on rock. When a flood came, a torrent struck that house but could not shake it, because it was well built. But the one who hears my words and does not put them into practice is like a man who built a house on the ground without a foundation. The moment the torrent struck that house, it collapsed and its destruction was complete."
Luke 6:48-49

Give Us Grace to Stand

He's building a foundation that never can be shaken,
with Christ the Cornerstone.
He's raising up a people underneath His steeple,
with Christ the Cornerstone.
Rocks of faith sustain it; nothing can defame it,
with Christ the Cornerstone.

Time is of the essence; God will surely bless us;
we stand on Solid Rock.
Praises to the Builder; with mortar He has sealed her;
we stand on Solid Rock.
A holy people risen, by His Spirit driven;
we stand on Solid Rock.

Bring us to fruition by Spirit's intuition;
give us grace to stand.
A people in your presence, brick by brick ascendeth;
give us grace to stand.
By your love to seal us, and by your mercy heal us;
give us grace to stand.

*"My hope is built on nothing less than Jesus' blood and righteousness.
I dare not trust the sweetest frame, but wholly lean on Jesus' name.
On Christ the solid rock I stand, all other ground is sinking sand."*
Hymn: My Hope is Built on Nothing Less, Text: Edward Mote, Tune: John B. Dykes

Josephine

how strange at first I thought
this child praying to a rock
could she not see,
devout heathen Cree,
a rock a God could never be?
that was before I remembered
barren Hannah declaring
"There is no God like our Rock,"

before the testimony of Moses,
"The Rock his work is perfect,"
before the echo of the psalms,
"O Lord my Rock and my Redeemer,"
before the recollections of Paul,
*"They drank from the supernatural Rock
which followed them,
and the Rock was Christ."*
before my confession of faith,
*"Built upon the foundation
of the apostles and prophets,
Christ Jesus himself
being the cornerstone"*

Oh not so strange I later thought,
little Cree on bended knee
waiting for her Paul on Athens Hill
to perceive a readiness for truth,
and stun the Areopagus
with wisdom from on high
and he came and named her rock

**Almighty
Redeemer
King of Kings
Jesus !**

"Paul then stood up in the meeting of the Aereopagus and said, 'People of Athens! I see that in every way you are religious...I even found an altar to an unknown God. So you are ignorant of the very thing you worship...The God who made the world does not live in temples built by human hands...Rather, he himself gives everyone life and breath and everything else...For in him we live and move and have our being.'" Acts 17:22, 23b, 24, 28 NIV

"And I tell you that you are Peter, and on this rock I will build my Church, and the gates of Hades will not overcome it." Matthew 16:18 NIV

Rock of Salvation

God the Rock of our salvation,
fortress of our captivation;
strong, unyielding, steady stone,
from which our struggling faith is born.

Him our stronghold destination,
where dwells the God of all creation.
Refuge and protective arm,
assuager of all earthly harm.

Strong deliverer of the nations,
offering us Christ's invitation.
Paid in full our sin and guilt;
on this our trembling faith is built.

Rock and fortress, gracious giver,
entwine our souls in thee forever.
Holy spirit, work of grace,
lift us up to see your Face.

"The Lord is my rock, my fortress, and my deliverer; my God is my rock in whom I take refuge, my shield and the horn of my salvation, my stronghold."
Psalms 18:2 NIV

Helmet Pigeons

The Polish Helmet or Polish Krymka Tumbler is a breed of fancy pigeon, specifically a type of Helmet pigeon that has been developed over many years of selective breeding. It is distinctive because of its "muffs" (large foot feathers), and is colored only on the top half of its head (the "helmet") and on its tail. It is thought to be related to the European and American pigeons, though it remains unknown as to what came first or how they spread and adapted all over the world.

Wikipedia contributors. (2018, March 27). Polish Helmet Pigeon. In Wikiipedia, The Free Encyclopedia. Retrieved 22:56, March 4, 2019,from https://en.wikipedia.org/index.php?title=Polish_pigeon&oldid=832685054

In Ephesians, Chapter 6, Paul instructs Christians on how to dress to do battle against the devil's evil schemes. Some of these include wearing a breastplate of righteousness (white is a good color); shoes, lighter than feathers, fitted with the gospel of peace; the HELMET of salvation; and the sword of the Spirit which is the Word of God. The fancy crest is the Cross, and selective breeding leads him into battle. He has everything he needs to be victorious! And…he won't have his hands (his wings, I mean) at his side. He needs them to raise the shield of faith. Onward Christian soldiers!

A Christian with a Mission

I'm proud to be a Christian with a mission;
I'm proud to be a soldier for the Lord.
I still uphold the teachings of the Bible;
I still believe it is the Word of God.

I'm proud to be a Christian with a mission;
I'm awed by every word my Savior said.
I still believe that victory is in Jesus;
With Christ alive, the church cannot be dead!

I'm proud to be a Christian with a mission;
I'm thrilled to wave the Gospel banner high.
I still believe his Kingdom is eternal;
I still believe I'll meet him when I die.

I'm proud to be a Christian with a mission;
I'm proud to serve the army of the Lord.
His armor always will protect me
As I battle with his double-edged sword.

"Finally, be strong in the Lord and in his mighty power. Put on the full armor of God that you can take your stand against the devil's schemes. For the battle is not against flesh and blood, but against the rulers, against the authorities, against the powers of this dark world and against the spiritual forces in the heavenly realms." Ephesians 6:10-12 NIV

"For the word of God is alive and active. Sharper than any double-edged sword, it penetrates even to dividing soul and spirit, joints and marrow; it judges the thoughts and attitudes of the heart. Nothing is hidden from God's sight." Hebrews 4:12 NIV

Forward into Battle

Don't go barefoot into battle;
shoe your feet with Godly peace.
Avoid the "spikes" that threaten
to rip and shred your feet.*

You will always meet with danger
when the enemy attacks;
Go forward with God's weapons,
and do not turn your backs.

How strange that shoes of peace
are contending now with swords;
but keep in mind your purpose;
know the battle is the Lord's.

Remember who you stand with;
Don't forget who called you forth.
Lace and tie your boots with courage;
With his Spirit, stay your course.

Soldiers in Bible times, and even earlier, faced an unforeseen danger in battle. Their enemies would pound spikes into the ground, and when they stepped on them, their feet were sliced open like a razor, causing great injury. Roman soldiers wore sturdy boots that were less likely to be punctured.

"Having shod your feet with the preparation of the gospel of peace."
Ephesians 6:15 NIV

Hope `a la King

Nuggets of hope are held captive,
Blocked by anxiety, fear.
When my future looks bleak;
And my joy sprung a leak,
Where did my hope disappear?

Is it hiding in pockets of pain, Lord?
Was it struck by the falcons of fear?
Did hope have a stroke,
Unknowingly choke,
While medics did not interfere?

My faith is not seeing the rainbows;
My hope is not driving the wind.
Come back to me, Lord,
Please drag me aboard;
Serve me your hope `a la King.

The Battle is the Lord's

We lug our heavy armor;
our mighty weapons wield.
We challenge our opponent
on some lonely battle field.

We may not hold a dagger,
or pull the trigger on a gun,
We can kill with vicious words;
wound until we've won.

Whether minor skirmish,
or major all out war;
we can't ignore the battle,
but the battle is the Lord's.

So, before you choose your weapons,
rehearse your wounding words;
remember, victory or surrender,
the battle is the Lord's.

"With him is only the arm of flesh, but with us is the Lord our God to help us and to fight our battles." 2 Chronicles 32:8a NIV

The Armor of God

I must now demand - be strong, so you can stand
firm against enemy schemes.
The Armor of God is never found flawed;
it shatters the evil one's dreams.

It wouldn't be right if the belt were too tight;
truth must have freedom to move.
Righteousness' plate must quicken the gait,
must be tight with victory to prove.

Make ready your feet with the gospel of peace,
and take up the shield of your faith.
Extinguish the darts aimed at your hearts,
Hell's fiery arrows of hate.

Take up the sword, fight with God's Word,
salvation's helmet will cover.
Steady in prayer, be always aware,
and fight the good fight like none other!

"Finally, be strong in the Lord and in his mighty power. Put on the full armor of God, so that you can take your stand against the devil's schemes."
Ephesians 6:1011 NIV

A Shell-tered Life

If I could be a turtle, Lord,
I'd crawl into my shell.
I'd shut out all my feelings, Lord,
and all my fears as well.

I'd put my arms around me,
beneath my turtle bark.
Perhaps, in time, I would become
accustomed to the dark.

I wouldn't see; I wouldn't feel,
nor sense the world outside.
If I could be a turtle, Lord,
I'd slip away, I'd hide.

Wouldn't I be happy, Lord,
so free from pain and strife?
**My child, I did not call you
To live a shell-tered life.**

"I have told you all this so that you may have peace of mind. Here on earth you will have many trials and sorrows; but cheer up, for I have overcome the world."
John 16:33 LB (paraphrased)

Save Us from this Hour

Afflictions,
Addictions,
Chase us in the night,
Stealing hope and courage,
Shutting out your light.

Afflictions,
Addictions,
These massive giants, tall,
Follow us and swallow us,
Make us stumble, fall.

Afflictions,
Addictions,
Are mighty in their power.
Only God Almighty
Can save us from this hour.

"It was good for me to be afflicted so I might learn your decrees. The law from your mouth is more precious to me than thousands of pieces of silver and gold."
Psalms 119:71-72

A Just Survivor

As I turn the curled pages
And I look beyond the print;
In gratitude I'm pondering
Just how your life was spent.

You were never welcomed warmly,
They dressed you in a cloak;
You were the talk of counsels
And withheld from common folk.

You were battered, burned and blistered,
hidden for a thousand years.
You were a book forbidden
By their emperors and seers.

Did they fear your words of wisdom?
Did they doubt the Spirit's power?
Why did they silence Scripture,
From their pompous ivory tower?

I turn your pages fondly
And I cherish every breath,
You are a just survivor
Of an ill-intended death.

"Heaven and earth will pass away, but my words will never pass away."
Matthew 24:35

Battle of the Mind

How can I serve you Lord
With a mind of purity?
How can thoughts of judgment
Stop rambling on in me?

I think and speak of love and grace
and total trust in Thee,
but hidden corners of my mind
Peek out in mockery.

I analyze; I theorize,
I try to sweep them clean
but dust seems always to return;
Why can't they always gleam?

Is a pure mind possible;
Can I love with ALL of it?
Then power up my spirit, Lord,
To strike offenders dead!

"As a man (woman) thinks in his/her heart, so does he/she become."
Proverbs 23:7 NIV (paraphrase mine)

Archangel Pigeons

The Archangel is a breed of fancy pigeon, notable for the metallic sheen of its feathers. Archangels, along with other varieties of domesticated pigeons, are all descendants from the rock pigeon. It is kept as an ornamental or fancy breed, valued for its unusual appearance. They have unfeathered legs and dark orange eyes. They may or may not be crested. The body of the bird is bronze or gold with wings that are either black, white or blue.

Wikipedia contributors, (2017, November 17). Archangel pigeon. In Wikipedia, The Free Encyclopedia. Retrieved 23; 37, March 4, 2019, from https://en.wikiapedia.org /w/index.php?title =Archangel_pigeon&oldid=810868750

God's created archangels were also arrayed with great majesty when they appeared to designated persons in biblical times. Archangel denotes an angel of high rank. The name of the archangel Michael means "prince" or "minister," thus explaining their mission as Christian counterparts.

"Are not all angels ministering spirits, sent to serve those who will inherit salvation?" Hebrews 1:14 NIV

Christmas Blessings

Christmas Day is fading
and in its passing, peace
that captures all my being,
all that love bequeaths.

I have been touched by angels,
raised up on sacred hymns,
embraced by words of Scripture,
all that Christmas brings.

Light has charged my spirit,
illumined truths so rare,
whispered promises of hope,
sealed with Simeon's prayer.

God's Son has spoken wisdom
that only faith can hold,
'til He comes again in glory
and reigns from pole to pole!

"For my eyes have seen your salvation, which you have prepared in the sight of all nations: a light for revelation to the Gentiles and the glory of your people Israel." Luke 2:30-32 NIV

"But Mary kept all these things, pondering them in her heart." Luke 2:19 RSV

Overanxious

Long after dawn
Hope rising
I hurry to the resurrection site.

Heart racing
Tracing the swollen creek
Heavy anxious feet
Snapping naked branches
Felled by winter storms
I seek the living among the dead.

Greedy, fumbling hands
Shake but cannot wake
Slumbering pussy willows

Sunlight dancing on bonneted brows
Cannot unravel flimsy grave clothes
Angels keep steady watch over silken splendor.

Determined to witness a resurrection
I arrived too soon
Angels were not ready
To fling wide the tufted tombs
Meanwhile I return
to my waiting room.

"I remain confident of this: I will see the goodness of the Lord in the land of the living. Wait for the Lord; be strong and take heart and wait for the Lord."
Psalms 27:13-14 NIV

Cowboy Boots in Heaven

Are there cowboy boots in heaven?
Are there trails beyond the skies?
Are there spurs to greater glories?
Then I know she's riding high!

Do the horses really glisten?
And can they really fly?
Are there golden belts and buckles?
Then I know she's riding high!

Are there saddles made of silver?
Are there steady reins to try?
Are there slopes to greener pastures?
Then I know she's riding high!

Are there silken manes and mantles?
Are there cowboy hats to buy?
Are there hoofs of solid ivory?
Then I know she's riding high!

Are there rivers ever winding?
Are there brooks that don't run dry?
Are there picnics with the Savior?
Then I know she's riding high!

Does a posse of God's angels
Ride before and death defy?
Can she touch the face of Jesus?
Then I know she's riding high!

In memory of Gina Germscheid who died much too young.

"Blessed are the poor in spirit, for theirs is the kingdom of heaven. Blessed are they who mourn, for they will be comforted…" Matthew 5:3-4 NIV

In Your Will?

I must know that I am in your will,
must know, must know, must know.
You sent angels to the ancients,
prophetic words bestowed.

You gave dreams to kings and nobles,
hieroglyphics on their walls,
messages in sand and soil,
your star in heaven's halls.

It's true I know your will, O God;
I've known it since a child,
but sometimes I've been "in"
and sometimes dwelt "outside."

So keep your banners waving;
send a message or a clue.
Reproof or reassurance
is what I need from you.

I love you and I need you,
but I'm confused right now.
My mind is playing tricks on me,
and I can't sort it out.

So tape a note upon my mirror,
where only I can see,
And when I'm seeing double,
it might be good for me!

"Be very careful then how you live—not as unwise but as wise, making the most of every opportunity…but understand what the Lord's will is…"
Ephesians 5:15-17 NIV

First and Foremost

First and foremost, front and center;
lift Him higher as we enter.
Place him in the highest sphere,
wondrous Lord, whom we revere.

Seek the things that are above you;
he alone is most high God.
Set your mind on things eternal;
don't let your joy the devil rob.

Higher, higher, always higher,
lift your hands and hearts in praise.
He'll support you with his angels;
you will see the heavens blaze.

"He will be raised and lifted up and highly exalted…"
Psalms 52:13B NIV

"Since, then, you have been raised with Christ, seek the things that are above where Christ is seated at the right hand of God." Colossians 3:1 NIV

Instant Gratification

Patience, Lord, I need it now;
Sweat is forming on my brow.
Confusion hovers over me,
Satan smiles; God help me!

Give me peace with patience, Lord.
Today is good, are you on board?
I'm in a hurry – no debate;
You know me, I hate to wait.

And while you're at it, give me grace;
And please, dear Lord, don't hesitate.
If you are busy, send your host
of angels flying coast to coast.

I'm awake by half-past seven;
can you make it by eleven?
My door is open as you know;
no need for you to walk tip-toe.

I'll be waiting in my chair
for ready answers to my prayers.
Cover me with patience, peace,
and extra measures of your grace.
I know this is no cup of tea.
You leaving now? Without a fee?

"We continually ask God to fill you with the knowledge of his will through all the wisdom and understanding that the Spirit gives, so you may live a life worthy of the Lord and please him in every way: bearing fruit in every good work, growing in the knowledge of God. Being strengthened in all power according to his glorious might, so that you may have great endurance and patience." Colossians 1:10-11 NIV

Doing the Polka in Heaven

Fill my heart with joy and let my spirit dance,
wondrous notes by you, Lord, be given.
Twirl me in your arms and set my soul to prance;
we'll do the polka in heaven.

Surrounded by your angels, halos shining bright,
lead me to drink of your splendor.
Orchestrate your instruments; tune them up just right,
music only heaven can render.

Sweep me down the avenues, through arches made of gold;
stun me with the jewels on your throne.
Dip me deep on steady notes that you forever hold,
dancing free without a chaperone.

Spin me 'round in circles and lift me off my feet;
myself, Lord, to you I have given.
Holding hands with Jesus and moving to the beat,
thrilling to the polka in heaven!

"Let them praise his name with dancing…" Psalms 149:3a NIV

"Wearing a linen ephod, David was dancing before the Lord with all his might…" 2 Samuel 14 NIV

King Pigeons

The King Pigeon breed is known for large size. It is a dual purpose breed originating in United States. It is called the "Snow King" to distinguish it from the purely utility variety which is raised for food. They were developed during the 1890's by crossing four older varieties: the Duchess for grace; the "Homer" for alertness; the "Maltese" for compactness and style; the "Runt" for body and size..

Wikipedia contributors, (2018, June 15). King pigeon. In Wikipedia, The Free Encyclopedia. Retrieved 02:25, March 10, 2019, from http://en.wikipedia.org/w/index.php?Title=King_pigeon&oldid=845912

Another King went to his death to take on the sins of the world. God raised him from the tomb on the third day, full of grace like the Duchess, alert to the needs of his disciples like the Homer, and well-packed, like the Maltese, with wisdom and instructions for his followers. Jesus is with us in life and also in death. He was, and is our risen Lord and King, living and reigning through all eternity!

Transcending Sound

What miracle of sound is this?
What language without word,
that bends my ear in accents clear,
yet silently is heard?
What syllables divide the heavens
to accent every star,
and without word, love's voice is heard
in echoes from afar?

What discourse covers all the earth
with breaths of virgin snow,
each voiceless flake proclaiming grace
to wintering souls below?
What oratory lifts each bough
of Christmas pine and fir,
with tongue-less ease delivers peace
and joy to all the world?

What elocution wings its way
O'er land and air and sea?
On muted crèche salvation stretched
from Bethlehem to me.

"When the angels had left them and gone into heaven, the shepherds said to one another, 'Let's go to Bethlehem and see this thing that has happened, which the Lord has told us about.'" Luke 2:15 NIV

You are My Everything

You are gracious; you are kind;
You're the Father of mankind.
Life and power you bring.
You are blessing; you are peace;
May your healing love increase.
You make my Spirit sing.

Lord of glory, King of Kings;
Comfort to my heart you bring,
Majesty on high.
You are wisdom; you are truth.
Your name I've known since youth;
my soul doth magnify.

You are my shield of faith,
I will always seek your face,
precious Prince of Peace.
You will sustain, provide;
In you I will abide,
Always first in line at your feast.

"And he will be called *Wonderful, Counselor, Mighty God, Everlasting Father, Prince of Peace. Of the greatness of his government and peace there will be no end,*" Isaiah 9:6b, 7a NIV

The Great I Am

You are the great "I Am", you are.
You are the Spirit, the Counselor.
You are the Lord, my Savior too;
You are my Guide in all I do.

You are my teacher every day;
You are the light, the truth, the way.
You are the Shepherd of mankind;
You are my life, the one true vine.

You are the resurrection too;
Guardian of my soul are you.
You are Bread of Life from heaven.
You're living water freely given;

You are the Father of Creation;
You are the Promise of Salvation.
You are the royal Prince of Peace;
You are the God of Righteousness.

The Great Physician, too, art thou.
You were then; you still are now.
The evening star, the blazing sun;
You are the blessed three in one!

Lord of Lords and King of Kings;
You are the reason my heart sings.
You are the beginning and the end;
Indeed You are my everything!

"God said to Moses,' I AM WHO I AM.' This is what you are to say to the Israelites: 'I am has sent me to you.'... 'This is my name forever, the name you shall call me from generation to generation.'" Exodus 3:14,15b NIV

Gathering Time

In the early morning hours
I wander aimlessly from room to room
mind racing
heart searching
swollen eyes resting on little things.

Indian corn encased in crackling husks
pumpkins in readiness for little hands
field flowers, weeds, and autumn leaves
empty corn fields framing my windows.

my favorite picture of Jesus
with sad, penetrating eyes
a "Give Thanks" wood carving from a student
and a time-worn plaque above my sink
"…except a grain of wheat
fall into the ground and die
it remains alone, but if it dies
it bears much fruit."

I am strangely blessed
by this mingling of earth and heaven,
this ever-present cycle of life and death
I know, Lord, I know;
it's gathering time.

"Though he brings grief, he will show compassion, so great is his unfailing love, for he does not willingly bring affliction or grief to anyone." Lamentations 34:32-33 NIV

stillborn syllables

today
we drive in silence
to the cancer center

An ominous quiet
choking
would-be utterances

stillborn syllables
paralyzed
by their own inadequacy
destined to die
in infancy

"But you, Sovereign Lord, help me for your name's sake; out of the goodness of your love, deliver me. For I am poor and needy, and my heart is wounded within me."
Psalms 109:21-22 NIV

Death

How I wish this were an assignment
I could choose
not to do

a meeting I could skip
an outing I could cancel
a project I could abort.

But death
is mandatory
requiring my attention
and my attendance;
she does not admit quitters
and I cannot call in sick.

"Who can live and not see death, or who can escape the power of the grave?"
Proverbs 89:48 NIV

"He will swallow up death forever. The Sovereign Lord will wipe away the tears from all faces." Isaiah 25:8 NIV

Running Free

I stared at the picture
for a long time,
wild horses
running free,
never meant for captivity.

Down the hall
in bed one,
another of your creation
longing to be free.

Yes, I know,
he never really
belonged to me.

Let him go, Lord,
turn him loose;
let him stretch
his legs
and run
Free!

"...The Lord has anointed me...to proclaim freedom for the captives and release from darkness for the prisoners..." Isaiah 61:1 NIV

Dustin

"Grandma,
I wish I were little again."

Was this really
my 7-year-old grandson
who was always convinced
that grown-ups have more fun?

I watched a tear
slide down his cheek.

"I wish I were little again
because then grandpa
would be here."

"Oh, me too, sweetheart,
me too."

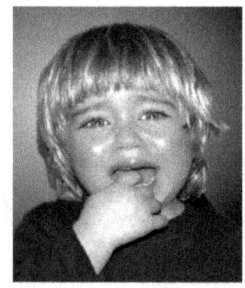

"Grandpas have ears that truly listen, arms that always hold, love that's never-ending, and a heart that's made of gold."
--author unknown

Molly

Her little arms
tightened around me
as she sobbed,
"but I'll never see him again!
Why can't Jesus just let him come back?"

There are no words
to explain death to a four-year-old,
and understanding does not come with age –
only more questions.

"He wasn't just my grandpa,
He was my friend."

I know, sweetheart,
I know.

"The cords of death entangled me, the anguish of the grave came over me; I was overcome by distress and sorrow. Then I called on the name of the Lord: 'Lord, save me!' The Lord is gracious and righteous; our God is full of compassion."
Psalms 116:3-4 NIV

Dustin and Molly

They stood before the casket,
boy of seven,
girl of four;
the younger comforting the older.

Facing her brother
and wrapping her small arms
tightly about him,
she looked up as if to say,
"Don't cry, Dustin, I'm here."

It didn't matter that her little head
came only waist high,
for her message
was much, much taller.

"Children of the heavenly Father, safely in his bosom gather;
Nestling bird or star in heaven, such a refuge ne'er was given.
Neither life nor death shall ever, from the Lord his children sever;
Unto them his grace he showeth, and their sorrows all he
  knoweth.
Though he giveth or he taketh, God his children ne'er forsaketh.
His the loving purpose solely to preserve them pure and holy."

Hymn: "Children of the Heavenly Father"
Text: Simon Browne, Tune: William Knapp

Brooding Silence

The house is silent
Your chair empty
I am alone.

A heavy
brooding
silence
that drags on the soul
and quenches the spirit.

A muffled cry of absence
designed only for my ears

"We are of good courage, and we would rather be away from the body and at home with the Lord…" 2 Corinthians 5:8a RSV

Sanctuary

Twisted and weather-beaten,
it lay buried in the snow and ice,
the feathered creatures long having fled
their summer home.

I carried it to the house,
embracing the barren wood,
once crafted by your hands,
now silenced by death.

This battered birdhouse
was empty, not silent.
It spoke tenderly
of other sanctuaries
created by your hands,
places of refuge
for all God's creatures.

And now it is you, who have fled,
finding sanctuary from your winter storm.
You have been made new
by a carpenter from Nazareth,
the dying work
of his nail-scarred hands.

"You, God, are awesome in your sanctuary; the God of Israel gives power and strength to his people." Psalms 68:35 NIV

Dark Winter

Icy tentacles,
grotesque twisting,
endeavoring to prolong
this dark winter
without and within.

These evil spirits hover
above my windows
whispering
and weaving
icy curses
of fear
inadequacy
and defeat.

Oh God!
Tell me this winter will end.
Tell me your love will triumph.
Tell me, O Lord,
please tell me
I will be whole again.

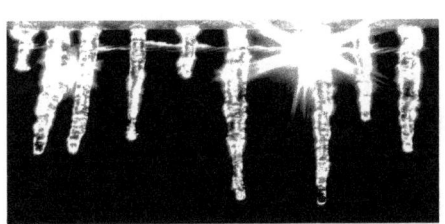

"The darker the night, the brighter the stars, the deeper the grief, the closer is God."
-Fyodor Dostoyevsky, Crime and Punishment

"There is no grief like the grief that does not speak." -Longfellow

Sharing Seeds

The female cardinal
searches the snow today
without her partner,
desperate for nourishment,
encircled by a faithful congregation of snowbirds
sharing their snow-covered table.
She is not alone.

I also search
for food today
without my partner,
knowing I am surrounded in prayer
by believers,
sharing their seeds,
drawing the circle of faith
and friendship
even tighter.
I am not alone.

"But if we walk in the light as he is in the light, we have fellowship with one another, and the blood of Jesus, his Son, purifies us from all sin." 1 John 1:7 NIV

"They all joined together constantly in prayer." Acts 1:14a NIV

Loaves and Fishes

Like loaves and fishes
They feed my emptiness.

I savor each photo
While listening,
Longing,
And reliving.

It is more than a meal –
It is a miracle.

And now
I must gather up
Leftover fragments
That nothing be lost.

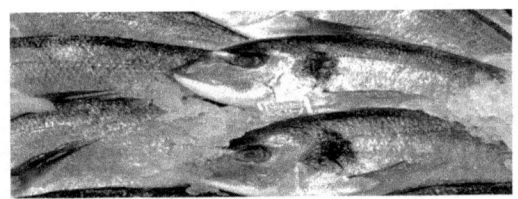

"For I was hungry and you gave me something to eat..."
Matthew 25:35a NIV

"The life of the dead is placed in the memory of the living." Cicero

Sprinkle Me Softly

The sky is raining
tiny tears
gently reminding me
of your absence.

They do not fall
in angry, icy torrents
as they once did,
but moist, glistening droplets
of hope and healing.

I throw back my head
and raise my hands
toward heaven,
anxious for God to sprinkle me softly
with the wonder of his love,
completing this circle of life in death,
death in life.

"Heal me, Lord, and I will be healed; save me and I will be saved, for you are the one I praise." Jeremiah 17:14 NIV

"Hope smiles from the threshold of the year to come, whispering it will be happier." - Alfred L. Tennyson

I Walked With Death Today

I walked with death today
down hospital halls
with whispering doctors, nurses on calls,
making their marks on patient charts,
smiling, smiling through it all.

I walked with death today,
x-rays, needles, untouched trays,
trembling lips, haunting eyes,
morphine glaring,
staring from him to me.

Oh, please, Lord, I do not wish to see
pain and suffering so near again,
the fading warmth of him
who did not feel my final touch.

It is too much for one short day
to live a year compressed in one,
spilling forth at will, and still,
yet, still, the light of advent shines;
indeed, it takes my breath away
and walks with me bereft,
walks with me in death.

"The saints, who here in patience, their cross and sufferings bore,
Shall live and reign forever when sorrow is no more.
Around the throne of glory, the Lamb they shall behold;
In triumph cast before him their diadems of gold."

Hymn: "Rejoice, Rejoice, Believers" Text: Laurentius Laurentii, Tune: Swedish folk tune

Slow Journey

Again surprised
at loneliness intense,
so far removed from death.

No sequence, I confess,
to love and loss;
no schedule nor calendar
to circle high and lows.

Death knows a pattern all its own,
a mystery on each page
of black and white,
braille replacing sight,
a journey slow,
and always chapters new
to write.

"I thought I could describe a state; make a map of sorrow. Sorrow: however, turns out not to be a state, but a process…for in grief nothing stays put. One keeps on emerging from a phase, but it always recurs. Round and round. Everything repeats. Am I going in circles, or dare I hope I am in a spiral? But if I am in a spiral, am I going up or down?" C. S. Lewis, A Grief Observed

Pouter Pigeons

The English Pouter is a breed of fancy pigeon developed over many years of selective breeding. English Pouters are all descendants from the rock pigeon. Historically, the English Pouter was also called the Pouting Horseman. The Pouter is long-limbed with an enlarged crop, and an overall large body. Charles Darwin described the English Pouter as being "perhaps the most distinct of all domesticated pigeons."

Wikipedia contributors. (2017). English Pouter. In *Wikipedia, The Free Encyclopedia*. Retrieved 02;01, March 10, 2019, from http://enwikipedia.org/w/indes.php?Title=English_Pouter&oldid=810869155

Christians can easily become puffed up like Pouters if not on their guard. There is a big difference between being exceedingly proud of our own accomplishments and being proud and excited about what God has done in our lives through the Holy Spirit. Jesus was never puffed up with pride, but always gave the credit to God the Father. He said that without the Father he could do nothing. Paul writes: "I have been crucified with Christ and I no longer live, but Christ lives in me. The life I now live in the body, I live by faith in the Son of God, who loved me and gave himself for me." God has given us all gifts, and prays that we use them for HIS glory. No more beating on our Pouter breasts. Puff yourselves up (or out) with His Holy Spirit!

Pouter Pigeons

We are Pouter Pigeons,
with our feathers puffed out wide,
spirit sometimes vain,
sinful self to blame;
we tumble on our ever present pride.

We are Pouter Pigeons
with our pulpits in the sky.
We preach,
we beseech;
quite often on the fly.

We, as Pouter Pigeons,
think we're better than the rest.
We've messages to carry;
we're more than ordinary.
We fly on high and sometimes beat our breasts.

"Look out how you use proud words. When you let proud words go, it is not easy to call them back. They wear long boots, hard boots; they walk off proud; they can't hear you calling—Look out how you use proud words." –Carl Sandburg

"Love is patient, love is kind. It does not envy, it does not boast, it is not proud." I Corinthians 13:4 NIV

When Did You Make Them That Way?

I'm finding that people are kinder;
I see more compassion each day.
They laugh and they smile, and life is worthwhile.
Lord, when did you make them that way?

I'm seeing more joy in their labors;
more indwelling peace every day.
Lord, isn't it strange that people have changed?
Just when did you make them way?

I've noticed that people are listening;
they care about things that I say.
Seems funny to me, Lord, don't you agree?
Why, YOU must have made them that way!

**"You say that people are different
And ask when I made them that way.
My child, it is grand, but you must understand,
it is you that I changed,
and not they.**

No Room

He listened and he sympathized
with the weary travelers' plea;
recognized their desperate plight
(Yes, he could plainly see).

He rationalized, apologized;
wished they'd come at noon.
Then feeling somewhat justified;
He firmly said, "No room!"

Lord, we, too, have listened,
were aroused to sympathy;
knew what we must surely do
to help someone in need.

We rationalized, apologized,
self-righteously assumed
that they were undeserving;
thus, we had no room.

"No room?" I hear him question;
"surely this can never be.
If your love comes with conditions,
then you've not made room for me.

I don't want a dusty corner
that's never seen a broom,
I'll knock until you answer,
"Come in, My Lord, there's room."

Here I am! I stand at the door and knock. If anyone hears my voice and opens the door, I will come in and eat with that person, and they with me...Whoever has ears, let them hear what the Spirit says to the churches. Revelation 3:20, 22 NIV

Crossed Emotions

I have a golden cross
with a tiny gold link chain.
I cannot wear it anymore;
it drives me near insane.

Fingers can't undo the clasp;
they fumble, bungle, botch.
How did it get all tangled
with agonizing knots?

Jumbles, jams, snarls and snags,
twists that won't undo.
How did they gang up on me?
Why do I fret and stew?

In desperation I withdrew
all efforts with my cross.
Again I tucked it in a drawer;
to me, it was a loss.

In defeat I bowed my head,
allowed my mind to wander.
God spoke to me in love,
urged my heart to ponder

all the wisdom, knowledge, truth
and power to untangle
all the fragile links of life,
every charm and bangle.

Emotions can become like knots
and do not glorify
God, who saved me in my sin
and seeks to sanctify.

Puffed up pride and prejudice,
raging words that wound,

Fear that shows I do not trust,
that brings upon me, ruin.

Love that only looks for gain
is not true love at all;
jealousy, hypocrisy,
leave stains upon the soul.

Quite like my twisted chain,
emotions tangle, too.
has power to defeat me;
sin sticks to us like glue.

His Spirit knows me like a book,
convicts my faulty flesh,
untangles moods to find the Cross
and chains of righteousness.

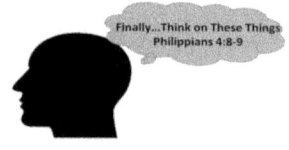

"Finally, brothers, and sisters, whatever is true, whatever is noble, whatever is right, whatever is pure, whatever is lovely, whatever is admirable, -- if anything is excellent or praiseworthy, --think about such things. Whatever you have learned or received of me, or seen in me – put it into practice. And the God of peace will be with you." Philippians 4:8-9 NIV

Consider the Pussy Willow

Consider the pussy willow
who refuses to be handicapped
by a back that will not bend,
or bemoan her existence
because she is not a dainty tulip
or a climbing rose,
smiling and taking bows
at the local garden club.

Even in her obscurity,
she reaches and rises
beyond the tulip and the rose,
as her soft silken fingers
impart grace to marshland magi.

She does not suffer identity crisis
or low self-esteem.
For her it is enough
to stand erect,
confident of her calling,
bowing only to the wind,
knowing it is enough
to touch,
enough to be free.

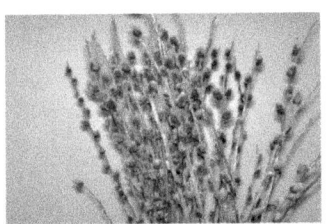

"If anyone thinks he is something when he is nothing, he deceives himself. Each one should test his own actions. Then he can take pride in himself without comparing himself to somebody else." Galatians 6:2-4 NIV

Pride

My Simon's pride needs sifting, Lord.

Sift it slowly that I might catch
and discard offending particles.

Sift it loudly
that I might hear
the Spirit's correction.

Sift it smoothly
that I might smother its vocal cords.

Sift it selflessly
that I may lay waste
the sin of self.

Sift steadily
with sanctifying hands.
And if I should boast,
may I boast only of Christ,
and Him crucified.

"A person may think his own ways are right, but the Lord weighs his heart."
Proverbs 21:2 NIV

"Those who guard their mouths and their tongues keep themselves from calamity."
Proverbs 21:23 NIV

sinking into self

stumbling through my stubbornness
falling on my pride
skinning knees with haste and waste
that never satisfy

leaves me lost and broken
sinking into self
find I'm not attending
to my spirit's inner health

stop your striving and conniving
set your pride aside
fix your eyes on Jesus
who will heal you from inside

let the Holy Spirit lead
beside the waters still
in gentleness and holiness
he will your portion fill.

"Do nothing out of selfish ambition or vain conceit. Rather in humility value others above yourselves, not looking to your own interests but each of you to the interests of the others." *Philippians 2:3 NIV*

Homing Pigeons (Homing, Racing, & Messenger)

The sport of flying (racing, messenger) Homing Pigeons was well-established as early as 3,000 years ago. They were used to claim the winner of the Olympics. Historically, pigeons carried messages only one way, to their home. They had to be transported manually before another flight. However, by placing food at one location and their home at another location, pigeons have been trained to fly back and forth twice a day reliably. Birds were used extensively during WW I. One homing pigeon, Cher Ami, was awarded the French Croix de guerre for her heroic service in delivering 12 important messages, despite having been badly injured.

Wikipedia contributors. (2019, March 2). In *Wikipedia, The Free Encyclopedia*. Retrived 05:11, March 10, 2019, from https://en.wikiapedia.org/w/indesphp? **Title =Homing _pigeon&oldid =885853128**

The Apostle Paul had many characteristics of the Homing, Racing, and Messenger Pigeons. From the time of his conversion he carried the Gospel of Christ to many corners of the earth, and endured many hardships along the way. When saying goodbye to the Ephesians, he said, "I only know that in every city the Holy Spirit warns me that prison and hardships are facing me. However, I consider my life worth nothing to me; my only aim is to finish the race and complete the task the Lord Jesus has given me—the task of testifying to the good news of God's grace." Jesus completed his task, when from the cross he cried out, "It is finished."

Ordinary People

God chooses common people; ordains them to go forth.
God uses common people for his kingdom's work on earth.
They may deem themselves unworthy; they may claim no gifts to go.
They may stammer and may stutter
like Moses long ago.

"I will equip you for the journey; I will slip you words of grace.
I will give you strength to follow as you daily seek my face.
I will wrap my Word around you; I will pack your bag with Faith.
I will travel close beside you;
I will keep you standing straight.
I won't leave you nor forsake you; I will weave my will to save.
I will treat you like a daughter; you will never be enslaved."

Servant, waver not your answer; servant, favor his request.
Servant, shake the dust that's clinging;
set forth at his behest.

Yes, my God, I'll go in earnest, with your banners flying high,
your promises to keep me strong, your angels set to fly.
With your blessing I will serve you; with your dressing I can stand.
I will labor for your kingdom;
please come and take my hand.

"He said to them, 'Go into all the world and preach the gospel to all creation. Whoever believes and is baptized will be saved.'" Mark 16:15-16 NIV

This poem was written for my granddaughter, Adrianna, before she went on a mission trip to Namibia in the summer 0f 2018.

Motherhood

Hands that once held the soft brushes of motherhood
Dripping with the aroma of home-made bread
Sticky with pancake syrup and popcorn balls.

Glistening in flight with needle and thread
Blending the rich colors
Of happiness and sorrow
Success and failure
Perfecting her strokes
Though sickness and health
Challenged by the artistry
Of the Master Painter.

Feet that once marched
To the disciplines of life
Blistered by the new shoes of widowhood
Weary from the weight of the great depression
Swollen from the heat of faithfulness.

Advancing when she might have retreated
Going the second mile
When every bone in her body ached
Keeping step to the steady beat
Of the Divine Drummer.

"Listen, my son (daughter), to your father's instruction and do not forsake your mother's teaching. They are a garland to grace your head and a chain to adorn your neck." Proverbs 1:8-9 NIV (Paraphrase mine)

The Postman Cometh

Signed, sealed, and delivered,
God's Spirit enroute to our souls,
stamped from on high with his glory,
burning with fiery hot coals.

Signed at the cross of redemption,
sealed with Christ's blood shed for me;
delivered on tongues sent from heaven,
fulfilling God's covenant decree.

Signed by the author, creator,
sealed with the wax of his Word,
delivered to all, stained by the fall,
God's letter of life undeserved.

"You yourselves are our letter, written on our hearts, known and read by everyone. You show that you are a letter from Christ, the result of our ministry, written not with ink, but with the Spirit of the living God, not on tablets of stone but on tablets of human hearts." 2 Corinthians 3:2 NIV

One Guest Room

Anger was absent from our house today;
love was invited to come and to stay.
We made her most welcome, tried hard to please;
cried when she started to pack up to leave.

Love gathered her things and when she was packed;
we peered out the window – saw anger was back.
We bolted the door to keep anger out;
pleaded with love to stay in our house.

Love wasn't happy, she wanted to stay;
didn't want anger to stand in her way.
We wanted love as a guest in our home;
we didn't want anger stealing her room.

Anger was pounding and kicking the door;
love didn't feel welcome with us anymore.
We had one invitation that we could extend
(anger and love could never be friends.)

We reached for love's hand and urged her to stay;
without hesitation, sent anger away.
She pouted and shouted and wanted to fight,
when we stood firm; she dropped out of sight.

"Do not make friends with a hot-tempered person, do not associate with one easily angered, or you may learn their ways and get yourself ensnared."
Proverbs 22:24-25 NIV

My Strength

My strength is yours, says the Lord of hosts;
One size of mine fits all.
I offer strength that cannot fail;
give courage to stand tall.

I'll give you sandals I have worn;
Try them, they will fit.
Shod with peace to greet each morn,
Strong and sturdy, will not quit.

Now rise and link your arm in mine;
Forget your wobbly knees.
I gladly give new strength to bind,
And raise you up like trees.

I'll give you words, magnetic,
To draw the hearts of men,
Inspired words, prophetic;
Words that do not bend.

You will know my total strength
Empowers your every step;
You will know the width and length
My promises have kept.

You have places now to go;
You have battles now to win.
Your strength will never be in doubt,
When you step into my skin.

"Blessed are those whose strength is you, whose hearts are set on pilgrimage. As they pass through the Valley of Baka, they make it a place of springs; the autumn rains also cover it with pools. They go from strength to strength, till each appears before God in Zion." Psalms 84:5-7 NIV

Fruit Patches

Love cuts and sews each tiny square;
Joy creates a pattern fair.
Peace secures the front and back;
Patience ties the quilt intact.

Kindness pins the outer edge;
Goodness hems with heavy thread.
Another gift of God to bless;
Followed up with faithfulness.

Before it's sent across the sea,
It's packed with great humility.
Godspeed blessed quilt to other lands,
The fruit of loving, willing hands.*

*Dedicated to the quilters, past and present, at St. Paul Evangelical Lutheran Church, Le Center. Minnesota.

"But the fruit of the Spirit is love, joy, peace, forbearance, kindness, goodness, faithfulness and self-control. Against such things, there is no law."
Galatians 5:22-23 NIV

Lost

I wrote a poem
with God alone;
in carelessness I lost it.
I searched computer files;
I sorted through the trash.
I paged through many books;
flipped through my paper stash.
But it was gone; I lost it.
Title was: "A Brand New Heart,"
In negligence I tossed it.

How many times have I been lost,
my mind not stayed on thee?
I could not find your righteous path,
your blessings far from me.
How many opportunities
are stilled beneath my hand?
How many words of truth and grace
are buried in the sand?

How many prayers are lost, unsaid?
How many hearts are broken,
because I lost my will to serve,
left healing words unspoken?
I cannot blame the enemy
for loss incurred by me.
I can't recover what is lost;
I CAN draw near to thee.

I wrote a poem "A Brand New Heart."
This heart by grace survives.
It was not lost, this heart of mine;
with joy it is alive.
With God alone, I wrote a poem;
It matters not its loss.
This brand new heart still lives in me;
Christ overcame the cross.

"Make the most of your chances to tell others the Good News. Be wise in all your contacts with them. Let your conversations with them be gracious as well as sensible, for then you will have the right answer for everyone."
Colossians 4:3-4 LB (paraphrased)

Without Restraint

We may pray on our knees,
batter God with our pleas;
lay prone in his presence each day.
We may learn of his will,
as we keep our voice still;
savoring His truth, and His way.

Our God may then command:
"Rise up, take a stand;
Deliver my good news to every land.
Baptize them in the faith;
keep your pathways straight.
You will help my kingdom to expand.

You are salt of the earth,
the flavor of new birth.
You can make disciples for the Lord.
I have sent you forth
to all corners of the earth;
I long for wandering souls to be restored."

Salt must not lose flavor;
store it in God's favor.
Take a salty stand, and do not faint.
Pour it out in fashion;
cover all the nations.
Do this willingly, without restraint.

"You are the salt of the earth. But if the salt loses its saltiness, how can it be made salty again? It is no longer good for anything, except to be thrown out and trampled underfoot." Matthew 5:13 NIV

The Wind Blows Where It Will

The wind blows where it wills; I hear and sense its power.
I try to stand at its demand but only do I cower.
It comes from the unknown and travels to the same.
I feel it surge; my spirit merge, but does it have a name?

I try to hear a still small voice that churns and churns within,
Try to discern the driven words, but can't hang unto them.
I strain; I fret, don't always get the sudden wind's intent,
And still don't know where it will go when all the rushing's spent.

I shudder at its turbulence; my heart observes with awe.
I watch it leave, yet can't conceive, of wind so right, so raw.
It came from where? A gift to share? I'm speechless in its wake.
Where did it go? I do not know. But I am wide awake!

"The wind blows wherever it pleases. You hear its sound, but you cannot tell where it comes from or where it is going. So it is with everyone born of the Spirit."
John 3:8 NIV

"and afterward, I will pour out my Spirit on all the people. Your sons and daughters will prophesy, your old men will dream dreams, your young men will see visions. Even on my servants, both men and women, I will pour out my Spirit in those days."
Joel 2:28-29 NIV

Dearest Babe of Bethlehem

We gather today to celebrate life,
but readily confess it has not always been abundant life.
We gather today to celebrate light,
but readily confess having walked in darkness more than light.

We gather today to celebrate family,
but readily confess the difficulty of celebrating with some chairs empty.
We gather today to celebrate birth,
but readily confess that the shadows of death still hover.

A poet asked: "Have we come all this way for birth or for death?"
Does death prepare us for life, or does life prepare us for death?
Why then do we feel so ill-equipped for both?

Dearest Babe of Bethlehem:
as we offer up the fragments of our life and death experiences,
and leave them beside your manger bed,
send us out into the world
with the same hope proclaimed by the angels,
the same trembling trust of the shepherds,
and the same marvelous light which drew the Wise Men
ever nearer to the Babe of Bethlehem.

"In Him was life, and that life was the light of all mankind. The light shines in the darkness, And the darkness has not overcome it." John 1:4-5 NIV

Nine-Eleven

A cross of twisted steel rises up amid the terror,
marking the graves of thousands,
America's answer to evil...
while smoldering fires still burn.

Flaming torches dissect the fallen beams,
crowded hospitals cradle the wounded,
families search for the lost...
while smoldering fires still burn.

Loved ones bury their dead.
Mothers, fathers, daughters and sons,
grandparents weep in the night...
while smoldering fires still burn.

Grief holds America hostage.
Well-meaning words have no power.
Sorrow brings a nation to its knees,
and raises it up with righteous resolve...
while smoldering fires still burn.

Those who sow with tears will reap with songs of joy. Those who go out weeping, carrying seeds to sow, will return with songs of joy, carrying sheaves with them." Psalms 126:5-6 NIV

Coming Home

Thank you Lord for earthly blessings,
wrapped in mercy, love and peace.
I have treasured every promise,
knew that you, your word would keep.

Somehow you kept me on the path,
rescued when I went astray.
You hid Your Word within my heart
to teach the truth, the life. the way.

You knew me in my mother's womb;
you loved me long before my birth,
prayed for me when just a child,
sought me when upon the earth.

Like a mother hen you gathered,
kept me safe beneath your wings,
gave comfort, strength and patience,
taught my spirit how to sing.

Now in the twilight of my years,
when my life has quickly flown,
I am not fearful of my death;
Dear Lord, I'm coming home!

From my Journal…

When I was a child, coming home was so many things. It was getting dressed while standing close to the oil burner on a very cold day…it was smelling homemade bread…it was knowing a mother's love…it was receiving mail…it was privacy…it was freedom to be myself…it was picking wild raspberries…it was going barefoot…it was reaching for the cookie jar. These were the comforts of home.

There were also discomforts: doing dishes…cleaning house, scrubbing floors…cleaning my room, doing homework…mowing lawn, pulling weeds…stripping wallpaper, hearing: "No", going to the dentist...doing a paper route, being confronted...being responsible.

A wise person once said: "It is not a journey into ourselves that we are undertaking, but a journey through ourselves so that we can emerge from the deepest level of the self into God." Coming home!

Footprints

Footprints leading from the hay,
widened by his grace each day.
Carefree foot prints taking us
through the streets of Nazareth.

Blindly, boldly, venturing forth,
leaving marks upon the earth.
Ordained, God's Kingdom to deliver,
footprints by the Jordan River.

Eager footprints gather more
by the Galilean shore.
Mighty marks on sand and sod,
footprints of the living God!

Footprints by his good friend's tomb,
footprints to the upper room.
Struggling to accept God's will,
He prays alone upon the hill.

Heavy footprints in the mud,
covered over by his blood.
A trail of tears forsaken, lost,
abruptly end beneath the cross.

Death is slow to righteous ruin,
But God is quick to empty tomb.
Holy, resurrected, free,
footprints calling "Follow me."

"It was time to leave—to say goodbye to Israel. I slipped from my steeple rock, sinking my bare feet into the sandy sea bottom, and walking slowly toward the shore. My footprints were quickly swallowed by the sea; his are forever preserved." From My Journal -1980

"He said to them all: Whoever wants to be my disciple must deny themselves and take up their cross daily and follow me." Luke 9:23 NIV